The Good, Bad, and The Ugly

The Untold Stories of a Spec Ops Sniper

Nicholas Irving

Copyright © 2022 Nicholas Irving

All rights reserved.

ISBN: 978-1-7367872-4-3

DEDICATION

This is dedicated to those who served during the Global War on Terrorism, and to the service members who continue to make sacrifices, so that we can continue to sleep peacefully at night. Thank you.

CONTENTS

	Acknowledgments	i
1	Prologue	1
2	The Summer of Love	Pg 7
3	Atropine	Pg 48
4	Molded for War	Pg 86
5	The Song of A Bird	Pg 125
6	Nothing Is Over	Pg 129
7	The Pattern	Pg 165
8	About the Author	Pg 196

ACKNOWLEDGMENTS

To those before me, and to those thereafter. RLTW!

PROLOGUE

"We knew the world would not be the same. A few people laughed, a few people cried, most people were silent. **Now I am become Death, the destroyer of worlds***. I suppose we all thought that, one way or another."*

I find the words of J. Robert Oppenheimer quite fitting when I find myself in my own mind, reminiscing about my time serving in special operations. Oppenheimer, an American theoretical physicist, is considered one of the fathers of the nuclear bomb during the Manhattan Project in the 1940s. His quote comes about after witnessing the first detonation of a nuclear bomb on July 16, 1945. On this date, the world witnessed the destruction caused by such a weapon on the testing grounds of Los Alamos, New Mexico. One month later, these devastating weapons of war would be detonated over the cities of Nagasaki and Hiroshima, Japan.

Within his infamous quote written in the opening of this prologue, Oppenheimer references a piece of Hindu literature, the Bhagavad Gita. Within this literature, Vishnu, a god, takes on his multi-armed form and reveals his true form to impress and convince the Prince that he should carry out his duty. And once Vishnu took on his true form, he says to the Prince, "Now I am become Death, the destroyer of worlds."

While my hands, nor those I served with, were credited with building one of the most devastating weapons in history, there is a shared sentiment. As members of the 75th Ranger Regiment, we were a part of an organization designed for a very particular task. Killing. We were dealers of death and destruction. We had to be. Molded through years of training and valuable lessons learned from men in the peculiar art of war.

Young men, some fresh out of high school, such as myself, were placed into an environment of chaos and havoc. Grade school mathematics, the sciences, history, and biology quickly became a thing of the past. Overnight, these topics were replaced and swapped out. Instead, we studied and mastered infiltration and exfiltration, target detection, and enemy elimination. And for our final exam and graduation, we would apply all that we had learned against men and women, who we never knew existed in foreign lands.

By the time I joined the ranks of the Ranger Regiment, serving in the 3rd Ranger Battalion in 2005, the men had been partakers of war for some time. A month after the September 11th attacks against the World Trade Centers and the Pentagon, the Rangers were deployed. Continuously, on a steady rotation, deploying every six months, members of the Ranger Regiment were taking the fight to the enemy. In fact, the Ranger Regiment was the only unit continuously deployed since the Global War On Terror campaign kicked off. On average, conducting over one-hundred special operations per ninety to one hundred and twenty-day deployment.

During our frequent trips to the middle east, we were credited with the death of tens of thousands of enemy fighters. Charred and destroyed remains are what we left in the territories we conducted our operations. Nevertheless, we were proficient in chaos and thrived when the cards stacked against us. Those who opposed us on battlefields rarely lived to tell their stories. Unable to share their tales of how they survived the devils with green, glowing eyes in the darkness of the night.

Our operations were fierce, brutal, and

struck with lightning-fast deadly precision. We became immune to the images that accompanied the hell that is war. Our nasal passages learned to adjust to the smell of burnt flesh from rockets that rained from the sky. Our vision, resistant to the sight of still, motionless bodies riddled with bullet holes from the projectiles we fired into them. And, our souls, callused. We were unaffected by the devastation we saw in the families and children of those we were sent to destroy.

We had become death. We were the destroyer of worlds. But that's who we needed to evolve into. To survive and thrive in a war-torn environment. So, I and those I served with became like a multi-armed beast, as Vishnu did to impress the Prince. One of our arms designed to kill. Another to strike fear into the hearts of our enemies. One to build an explosive charge to breach the home of those we were tasked to hunt down. Another limb to care for the lives of those that we considered brothers. And another limb to shield our loved ones back home from the trauma we had seen.

One limb we used to pull the strings of our emotions to form a smile. Another to cry. An arm to hug a fallen comrade as they took their last breath. And one to shove our own pains and tuck them in the depths of our souls that we felt inside. With these limbs, we not only destroyed the worlds of others, but we also demolished portions of reality within ourselves. Thankfully, a reality that an exceedingly small percentage of Americans will ever witness or experience.

Like the words of Oppenheimer, I suppose that we all feel this, one way or another. Only now, we are faced with a sort of dilemma. The destruction and death we once bore witness and caused, we now find ourselves trying to gather the pieces to rebuild and revive. At least, that is the hope that we can find to hold onto as we sort through the rubble we left behind within each one of us.

The Summer of Love

After completing the mandatory fourteen-week basic training and infantry school, airborne and Ranger selection, I was officially assigned to 3rd Ranger Battalion of the 75th Ranger Regiment. Soon after that, around six months, I would find myself deployed conducting special operations throughout various parts of Iraq. Particularly around and near the hometown of Saddam Hussein, in a city called Tikrit. Despite the terrorist leader being captured a few years before I arrived in the country, there was still plenty of fighting and terrorist activity in the area.

It was the summer of 2006. During this timeframe, US troops faced some of the heaviest resistance. Saddam Hussein was found guilty of war crimes and sentenced to death by hanging. The death of Al-Zarqawi, which led to the rebranding and forming of his terror cell into what we know today as IS, also took place in 2006. I was there during the height of it all. My unit even played a small role in the mission that killed Zarqawi.

I was as gung-ho of a new Ranger as they came. Eager to learn new things and be a part of any operation with which we were presented. Although it was my first deployment, it didn't take me long to get into the groove of things. I wanted to get my feet wet as soon and as much as possible. It had been a lifelong dream of mine to be doing the high-speed operations we were running.

"Get it on, boys! We got ourselves a target!" I heard one of the assault team leaders, Staff Sergeant Cort, shouting from outside my room. His pager chirped loudly and displayed a string of numbers as he made his way to the TOC (Tactical Operational Command). Depending on the numbers shown on the pager, they represented the priority of the mission. By the tone of SSgt Cort's voice as he yelled out to his team, I could tell the mission was one of high priority.

The TOC was a small room on our secluded compound, constructed of plywood and thick two-by-four beams. It was here that we'd receive our mission briefs and plan our actions on the objective. It was outfitted with state-of-the-art computer systems, large sixty-inch flat TV screens, and a few desks and satellite phones. Due to what took place here, lower enlisted guys, such as myself, tended to stay away.

"Irv!" Gonzalez, my team leader, shouted as he stuck his head into my room. I could make out the outline of his body as it silhouetted against an Iraqi sunset backdrop. He was wearing his body armor while carrying his ballistic helmet in one hand and his M4 rifle in the other.

"Yes, Sergeant?" I quickly and enthusiastically responded. Gonzalez never made it a habit to pay my room a visit, especially in full combat attire. So, there were only two reasons why he would have done so. He was informing me that I'd be joining him on the operation. Or me being the new guy, he needed me to grab him a plate of food while he was getting ready.

"Knock the crust out your eyes and get your shit ready to go. We need a couple of gun teams on this mission, so I'm choosing you and Mitch's gun team to head out with us. It's a good one, and you'll learn a lot from it. So, hurry up and meet me in the TOC. You have two minutes, or I'm leaving your ass to stay back and do pushups until we touch back down. Roger?"

"Roger Sergeant!" I responded, tripping over my unlaced boots and grabbing the assault pack full of machine gun ammo that I kept next to my bed.

I carried all of my mission essential gear as I made my way over small rocks that layered the ground in our compound and towards the TOC. It was like I could taste and smell the excitement in the warm, summers night air. Thirty-five or so young men, all Rangers, hurrying towards the TOC, decked out with everything they would need to wreak havoc on an unexpected enemy.

We were divided into five teams. Tagging along, we had our four-legged partner, a military K9 dog, Woodan. Three assault teams, which we referred to as squads, and two machinegun teams, mine and Mitch's. Mitch had several deployments over me. Two to Afghanistan soon after the invasion and once to Iraq a year before I arrived at the unit. He served years on a three-man machine gun team, working his way up through the team's positions. Everything from ammo carrier to machine gunner, and then on to team leader.

The majority of the missions we conducted were usually under cover of darkness. Being such a small-sized unit, working at night was one of our greatest allies. Not your typical conventional force, which is often deployed during daylight hours with fifty to one hundred men.

"Irv, we're over here," Gonzalez announced, waving me over to where he and Mitch's gun teams were. They were standing just outside the main entrance to the TOC, holding a folded, laminated map in hand. "We're about to go in and get the commander's brief. From what we know so far, it will be a good one and should be over quickly," he continued.

As we began piling into the TOC, I noticed the imagery displayed on the three large flatscreens. It was a live overhead feed from multiple air assets flying overhead of what I assumed to be the target we were planning to hit. These flying assets were usually unmanned drones. For hours, they flew tens of thousands of feet above a given location in a circular pattern. These eyes in the sky could conduct multiple operations throughout the day. Sometimes weeks, depending on the nature of the target.

Whatever these silent drones laid their high-definition camera lenses on, we received a live stream from its view. Moreover, these eyes in the sky could view a target with their infrared cameras, even in total darkness. So, there wasn't much that a terrorist could do to outrun or hide from our air assets.

"Alright! Listen up, men," Our commander, Captain Louis, announced in his baritone voice that carried a southern twang, walking towards a wooden podium front and center of the TOC. Louis stood a couple of inches over six feet tall and had the appearance of an NFL linebacker. Captain Louis was on the larger side regarding your typical Ranger, short and compact in size. I always found it amusing thinking of what he must have looked like jumping out of the small side door of a C-17 cargo plane. I imagined it similar to watching some sort of a magic trick, like watching a magician pull a rabbit out of his top hat.

He was an intimidating individual to anyone who hadn't spent some time with him. But, once you brushed past his rugged, war-battered figure and stern facial expression, that never seemed to alter. Captain Louis is what I had imagined a commander to be. He always put his men before the mission and could care less about the medals or accolades. Instead, he took care of the Rangers under him and ensured we had what we needed to accomplish the mission.

"We've been tracking this target for a while now. Based on the target's actions, we believe it to be a pit stop for foreign fighters coming into the region to fight." Captain Louis announced while glancing back at one of the screens behind him of the live footage.

The feed showed a single building in the middle of the desert. Surrounding the one-story building were sporadic growing shrubs and trees. From someone who hadn't seen how the enemy worked firsthand, the imagery wasn't what you'd expect as a place harboring terrorists. Although, a single structure or mud hut in the middle of nowhere land was the target we grew accustomed to hitting. Its innocent appearance and location were a prime spot for bad guys to conduct their business.

From my experience being on the ground, behind enemy lines, it was a rarity that we ever encountered Iraqi fighters. Instead, we often went toe to toe and exchanged hot lead with foreigners. Soldiers are paid by Iraqi terror organizations such as IS and Al Qaida to come in and do their fighting in exchange for currency. These foreigners came in from various parts of the middle eastern region, such as Syria, Sudan, and Egypt. The majority of the foreign fighters we encountered were Jordanian mercenaries.

"So far, from what we're able to determine since tracking this target, the opposition should be minimal. We've seen two MAMs (military-aged males) that live inside the building at any given time. One will leave in the morning hours in a flatbed Hilux pickup truck, while the other MAM stays behind and makes brief phone calls. We believe the calls he's making are in coordination with his buddies across the border. Perhaps giving them intel as to what entry points into the region are safest to traverse. Only on a couple of instances did we see both traveling together outside the building. When they did, it was a short-lived journey." Captain Louis continued with his brief. He made sure to give us as much information as possible after establishing the target's pattern of life.

Every eye in the room was glued to a screen studying the steady stream of the drone streaming in. Not a single Ranger showed the slightest bit of nervousness or concern. On the contrary, from the newest guy to those who have done this since the war kicked off. Everyone seemed as cool as a winter's breeze. But, of course, it's what I expected. Especially having seen them work over the past two months.

This deployment was what we coined to be "*The Summer of Love.*" From listening to some of the more seasoned guys' stories from previous overseas trips, this 2006 trip stood out drastically. Our deployment was anything short of combating boredom until this point. And far counting the days until we were heading back home to see our loved ones.

The Summer of Love was a three-month blood bath. For the enemy, that is. Ninety days of pure controlled violence against any advisory who stood in our way. Violence is something that I learned quickly that Rangers were really good at doing. Of course, we weren't shy about showing how good we were at it either. Within ninety days, we conducted countless direct action missions. More precisely, over one hundred of them, and no different from the one we were gearing up for tonight.

These fast-paced operations were all about bringing the fight to the enemy. We normally conducted direct action operations, or raids, involving killing or capturing the enemy. There was no in-between, and our rules of engagement were as clear as crystal. These raids didn't last long, spanning a few minutes to a few hours. However, regardless of the amount of time we spent on the objective, our results were undoubtedly highly effective.

"Tonight's operation, code-named Simpson, will take place outside the city limits you've all become familiar with. About a thirty-minute bird flight from here and over some gnarly terrain. Although, there shouldn't be any need for you to fast rope in. From its looks, you all should be able to land on the X and walk right into the front door." Captain Louis announced, indicating that the helo pilots would be able to land us within close proximity to the target building. I imagine that we all looked like packs of wild dogs that hadn't been fed in weeks, and this mission was like a T-bone steak. Being able to land that close to the target and not walk for miles was the mission we enjoyed the most.

"I know you're all ready to get it on. And I know you all have been at it day in and day out, sometimes two or three missions a night. However, don't allow your guys' success to become your complacency. And as always, be suspicious of your surroundings. Even though we suspect these turd eaters to be foreign fighters, let's be sure to keep the threat of IEDs in the back of your minds. Making IEDs may be part of their terrorist resume for all we know." Louis continued before dismissing us and headed towards an open area outside behind the TOC. A space large enough to hold the assault force and three Blackhawk helicopters for the night's raid. This staging area also served to keep us out of wondering, spectating eyes.

Exiting the TOC, we began forming up into our respective assault and machinegun teams. In the distance, I could already start to make out the distinct, muffled thumping of Blackhawks' rotor blades ripping through the night sky. It was a sound that, over the months, I came to have somewhat of a love and hate relationship with.

I hated it because it meant we were about to embark into the unknown and have yet another dance with fate. Regardless of the number of missions I've been on, there was never a guarantee that we would make it back. I don't care who you are or how tough you believe yourself to be. There is always a fear in your mind before heading out into harm's way. If there wasn't any, I'd question your emotions and rationality as a human.

However, I loved hearing those same rotor blades during an Exfil from a hostile location. Although we weren't considered out of harm's way until back at our base, getting on the helo meant we were one step closer.

"Let's go over all your shit and make sure you're not forgetting anything, Irv." Sgt. Gonzalez said, adjusting the night vision goggles attached to his helmet to see my equipment.

"Gun. Two hundred rounds in the sack on the gun. Belt ammo in your assault pack. NODs (night optic devices). Water." Gonzalez went down his mental checklist, placing a hand on everything he called out. As my team leader, he wanted to make sure there wasn't any doubt that his eyes were deceiving him. Gonzalez wanted to make sure I had everything and left nothing behind. His reassurance wasn't reserved for just the new guys either. Every Ranger had their equipment double-checked by another Ranger before heading out on a mission. Pre-mission excitement has been known to cause even the most seasoned guys to forget something at one point or another.

As Gonzalez finished his equipment checks, the silhouette of three Blackhawk helicopters appeared in the distance. They flew in, approaching us in a triangle formation low to the terrain. As they landed, the rotor wash of all three helicopters kicked fine dust and debris into the air. As well as into any bodily orifices or equipment that weren't properly covered.

To be the best, we had to fly with the best. Pilots of the 160th Special Operations Aviation Regiment (SOAR), also known as Night Stalkers, lived up to that description in every way imaginable. The soldiers who fill the ranks of Night Stalkers are well recognized for their proficiency during night operations. Since nearly one-hundred percent of our missions were under cover of darkness, the 160th was our go-to means of transportation. While known for their night capabilities, these soldiers were also recognized for their unparalleled precision. Where the average pilot would shy away from a landing, 160th was able to land in about any situation or terrain.

These helicopters were unlike what the conventional army guys used. Each was gutted out, free from seats, benches, and side doors. Being free of any chairs left more room for special operation soldiers to pack into the aircraft's center. And the lack of the helicopter's doors allowed us to sit along the side with our legs dangling out. As a result, each Blackhawk could easily fit an assault squad plus a gun team. And, while not as pleasant of a ride, it could cram more if the mission called for it.

"You strapped in, Irv!" Gonzalez shouted as we loaded the aircraft. Ensuring that I secured myself to the aircraft's interior with a safety bungee I had attached to a belt loop in my combat pants. There have been a few accidents where guys have fallen out. It's nearly impossible to hear anything less than a yell over the sound of the helicopter's rotors spinning overhead and its turbine engine.

Shouting was the only means of communicating.

Gonzalez and I sat in the aircraft's open doorway. My favorite spot whenever possible. Sitting along the side meant that I would be one of the first to have eyes on the target building as we approached the objective. Even looking through my NODs, the view wasn't bad either. I often found a serenity that accompanied flying through the night sky, moving close to seventy miles per hour. It was the only chance I got to take a moment before the mission was underway.

The flight was uneventful. Besides the pilots testing their countermeasure devices and flares to counter an incoming surface-to-air missile or rocket, it was a quiet ride. The area appeared just as boring in the distance and beneath my feet, flying a few hundred feet above. I was always torn between the environment around me and the actions within it. It was always hard to grasp that such a beautiful place could be filled with people that wanted nothing more than to kill me if given the opportunity.

"Ten minutes!" One of the pilots shouted aloud and over the Blackhawk's internal communication headsets. Everyone seated inside immediately relayed the time to target, ensuring we all got the message. The ten-minute mark was also the point we all went over our gear one last time, making sure everything was in its proper place and ready for action.

I could hear my heart begin to thump a little harder. Blood coursing through my arteries was like a stream of water beating against a bed of rocks, dampening the sound of the rotor blades above.

"Five minutes!" The second time mark echoed throughout the aircraft. Gonzalez looked towards me, extending his fist for me to pound with mine. Even in such dimly lit conditions, I could still see excitement peering through his green-lit eyes caused by the light in his night vision.

"One minute!" The time callouts continued, leading up to our thirty-second mark. Then, seconds before landing, the pilots flared the nose of the aircraft high into the air. They wanted to give us as soft of a landing as they could.

Before touching down, I caught a glimpse of the target building and its terrain. Everything appeared just as it had from the overhead imagery, we saw in the TOC during the mission briefing. A desolate landscape with a few sporadic growing vegetation and trees. Located in the midst was a single, one-story structure made of dried mud and rock. A light blue-colored Toyota Hilux pickup truck was parked in front, less than thirty feet from the exterior of the building.

The Hilux truck was nothing out of the ordinary. A common vehicle, driven often by the locals in the region. A durable, stick-shift truck that could easily haul materials and food over rough terrain from one location to another. On occasion, the enemy would use these vehicles to transport reinforcements or fighting equipment.

"GO! GO! GO!" Gonzalez shouted as he unlatched himself from the Blackhawk and exited with me following close behind.

All three of our helicopters nearly touched

down in unison and surrounded the target on three sides. However, they remained on the ground for only a few brief seconds. Barely enough time to get out and fight our way through the dust kicked up from the hurricane-force winds the helos produced. Then, as quickly as they landed, all three of the Blackhawks were back into the air. They each flew to a staging location that was relatively safe and minutes away from where they dropped us off.

It was understandable that the pilots didn't want to stick around longer than they needed to. The pilots were always adamant about how fast we needed to get out of the helo during training. A large, loud aircraft sitting stationary on the ground was prime picking for the enemy. Even as horrible as the enemy tended to shoot, it didn't take much skill to hit one.

The assaulters, carrying M4 assault rifles, sprinted towards the building. They used their infrared lasers and floodlights as they ran and shined them onto the building and the parked vehicle. Their lasers, which were only visible under night vision, now oriented at the target, turned the night into day. It was as if a ray from the sun shined from their weapons and illuminated the building. Every nook and cranny was exposed, leaving the enemy no place to potentially hide.

My machinegun team veered from the assaulting forces and headed towards the west of the target building. From one of the other Blackhawks, the second gun team briefly tailed behind us before heading towards the rear of the building. The main function of our teams was to prevent the enemy from fleeing the target. These fleeing personnel was what we referred to as *squirters*. Our job was to stop them before they somehow managed to escape before the assault teams gained entry.

From where we landed to the building, the total distance we had to move was less than a football field's length. Considering that we could cover that distance in less than a minute, it wasn't too far. Plus, having this much space between us and the target would give us a tactical advantage if the enemy decided to start shooting.

As Gonzalez and I neared our position, I looked toward second squad. They were the main assault force and now coming up on the blue Hilux. The team approached in a V-shaped formation, with twenty feet between each man. A building that allowed good visibility instead of walking one behind the other. In addition, having a twenty-foot separation allotted them some safety from enemy grenades. An explosion from a typical fragmentation grenade has a kill radius of five meters. A little more than sixteen feet. Although, the potential for catching shrapnel covered a much greater distance of around fifty feet.

"Arfae Yadayk!" The team leader of second squad, Sgt. Cortez shouted. He was giving a command in Arabic that translates to *Hands up*!

Cortez's laser pointed at the truck's flatbed. Less than a second after, six infrared laser beams from the rest of his assault force focused on the same location. My focus stayed on the team as they slowed their pace to a steady walk with their rifles shouldered. While I couldn't see what Cortez and his team were pointing out, I knew they spotted someone nearby.

"Hand's up, mother fucker!" Now, in a violent and authoritative tone, Cortez began shouting his commands in English. A few of his team men began to frantically echo the order and spread out even further. Then, finally, I could make out the silhouette of a human head that peeked from the truck's bed. Multiple lasers from the assault team stuck to the figure like magnets on a refrigerator.

Second squad was now less than twenty yards from the truck, still giving commands in Arabic and English. The slightly obscured head bobbed up and down, resembling a buoy in turbulent waters. It was as if he were trying to not be seen and frightened by our voices in the dark. Regardless of how harmless the unknown individual's actions may have appeared, it rarely ever turned out to be that way.

"Hands…" Like a bolt of lightning, a bright

flash abruptly interrupted Cortez's command. A split second after, a loud, near defining bang followed. The sound was loud enough that it caused my electronic hearing protection to momentarily shut off. Then, an unforgettable thud smacked against my body, nearly causing me to fall backward. The impact pierced through my body armor's hard plates, cutting through like a hot knife through butter. But that was nothing compared to what I saw happen to second squad.

Cortez's assault team briefly became engulfed by the bright flash. It was like I was watching a movie at half speed. Each man from second squad lifted off the ground and feet into the air, sending them flying rearward. They looked like ragdolls, tied to a string as their bodies hurled around and smashed back onto the Iraqi desert surface. By now, we all knew what had just taken place.

While lying in the truck, the man set off a suicide vest, exploding and instantly killing himself. And while I heard about these devices, it was the first time I'd seen the enemy firsthand employ such a devastating tactic. Throughout the war, the enemy became bolder in using suicide vests. They were often used as a last-ditch, one last hoorah, if you will, to kill as many people as possible.

The explosion sent a shockwave in all directions, impacting everyone on the ground. Visually, what I was seeing, didn't make much sense to me, if any. During our mission briefing, the threat of suicide bombers was never mentioned. The likelihood that we had encountered such a threat was minuscule. Especially when the greatest danger we faced was IEDs and small arms fire until this point.

As I'm sure most of us were, I was expecting calls for our medic to help tend to second squad, who more than likely took casualties.

"Fuck!" Gonzalez spoke aloud as he kneeled behind me, watching the scene unfold. His one-word expression, a sentiment that we all felt, interrupted an awkward and confused silence that settled amongst us after the explosion.

After such a violent attack, hearing absolutely nothing was rare in our line of work. One of the best responses to an enemy attack in training and combat was always to return the favor. Typically, we would respond by delivering an overwhelming amount of firepower, using everything we had in our arsenal. Overwhelming the enemy with such violence, they were stunned into submission, even if for a brief moment.

As the second squad lay on the ground, some grimacing in pain, first squad now began making their way to the building. First squad, also an assault force, was originally supposed to support and facilitate second squad while on the objective. They never missed a beat as they sprinted towards where the explosion had just taken place. While it was something that we trained for, we never expected it to happen. Rather than allow the enemy to gain the upper hand, first squad would have to take up the role of seconds.

Then, suddenly, the unmistakable sound of

an enemy PKM machine gun began emitting from the target building. The PKM is a Soviet-designed, belt-fed machine gun that fires a devastating 7.62 caliber round. It was one of the enemies' preferred weapons of choice, after the notorious and reliable AK-47, and has seen action in every major conflict since the late 1940s.

Watching first squad begin making their way into the building, rounds from the PKM began firing at its main entrance. Then, as if I thought the events during our night raid couldn't get any worse than they already were, Spc. Teal, one of the newer guys, suddenly collapsed and fell backward as he stepped in and cleared the doorway. Having seen the same bodily motion happen to our enemy, I didn't have to use my imagination to know what I witnessed.

According to our intel, there was still another MAM inside the building. Having a machine gun oriented towards the door was their last defense measure if allied forces were to try and enter. Alerted by the loud explosion outside, he knew we were near and decided to open fire. As the individual inside began firing, one of the bullets struck Spc. Teal in his helmet, knocking him unconscious and to the ground. A fail-safe method, firing blindly at the main entrance, to hit whoever was entering. One that was impossible for us to know in advance, let alone defend against.

While Teal lay on the ground, his squad continued on and into the structure, never missing a beat. Sounds of the assault teams returning fire from suppressed weapons instantly muted the barrage of fire from the PKM.

"One EKIA, firing from a position near the rear of the building." Sgt. Cortez's voice came in over the comms. "One wounded took a round to the head, but he's up and moving. Continuing to clear." He continued.

Thankfully, it turned out that the round that struck Teal was only enough to take him out of the fight for a brief moment. But, if anything, it stunned him. The bullet impacted the side of his helmet before ricocheting harmlessly away. This wasn't the first incident where an enemy round hit someone in the helmet. And they not only lived to talk about it but continued on with the mission. This was a testament to the quality of our equipment. It also displayed one's willpower and determination to stay in the fight. Regardless of rank or time on a team.

"This is M-12. Making my way towards second squad!" Our platoon medic, Doc Leo, M-12 being his designator, announced over our comms in an understandably frantic voice. His sole purpose was to treat and take care of anyone if they were wounded. And some of his best friends were in second squad who were blown up.

However, as he made his way to the downed men, they began rising back on their feet and gathering themselves. It was like watching a six-man team arise from the dead, shaking off dust and debris from their eyes and clothing.

"Everyone good to go?" Sgt. Cortez shouted out to his team.

"Roger Sgt! We're good. I guess the son of a

bitch didn't want us to take him out of his misery for him." One of the team leaders responded, then followed by a confirmation from each man on the team that they were able to continue on.

"M-1, this is M-12. Second squad is good. There are a few cuts, bruises, burns, and headaches, but I think they'll be fine. I'll take a closer look at each one once the objective is secure." Doc Leo announced to our ground force commander, SFC. Munn.

"Good shit!" Gonzalez said under his breath, still kneeling behind me, watching the situation unfold. Finally, after a rough, hectic start, the assault teams were gaining control. "Irv, keep the machine-gun oriented towards the west and make sure no one tries sneaking up on our guys." He whispered at me as I lay on my belly behind my gun. Having seen what I assumed was an entire team perish before my eyes, I didn't want to let the team down by not providing overwatch.

The smell of burning diesel fuel, sulfur, and cordite, filled the air and nearly overwhelmed my nostrils. I could also make out the faint scent of copper in the atmosphere. A tail sign of blood. This must have come from the suicide bomber after blowing himself up. His body parts littered the area where he detonated and scattered on the ground around. While disgusted, I felt relief that the scent of blood and burning flesh weren't any of our guys.'

The sounds of gunfire stopped almost as soon as they began. Once first squad shot the MAM operating the PKM, there were no threats to be engaged. We knew from the intel we received, back at base, that there were only two individuals who lived in the building. The PKM shooter and the suicide bomber should have been the only resistance we would face that night. Once all enemy threats were neutralized, the assault teams could continue gathering what the enemy may have left behind.

But that's the funny, strange thing about any intelligence. While we needed to receive it, it was never one-hundred percent certain, and what's reported is never set in stone.

Pop…Pop, Pop!

"One EKIA. Multiple MAMs, moving towards the black side of the objective." Sgt. Cortez, again, broadcasted over comms. He had shot another enemy threat while the assault teams continued to clear the building.

"That makes three?" The ground commander asked, ensuring that the number of enemy combatants was correct.

"Roger that. Three EKIA, with multiple MAMs exiting the building. My squad will be in pursuit." Cortez replied.

"Hells yes! We're up to bat, Irv. You see, you're free to engage anyone of these fuckers with a weapon. Make sure you identify your targets and don't confuse Cortez's team with any bad guys." Gonzalez instructed me. I could hear the excitement in the tone of his voice as the situation appeared that we may have a chance to get involved in the action.

Being on a machine-gun team had its perks at times when the opportunity arose. Our job was to keep the perimeter secure and watch out for squirters fleeing the objective during an operation. Being outside a targeted building usually kept us away from the heaviest fighting. As a result, the chances of engaging a target were slim, and they rarely presented themselves. However, those odds increased in our favor when a mission began to unravel, such as tonight. So, you could imagine the excitement that came over the gun teams, finally able to contribute to the violence we trained for months and years to master.

I took on a firm grasp of the pistol grip on my MK-48 belt-fed machine gun and pulled it tight into my shoulder. The whites in my knuckles must have looked like lightbulbs from the lack of blood as I gripped the weapon tighter. While it wouldn't have been the first time I shot a target, I had had a few by then, but my body still went through an emotional roller coaster. Being such an unnatural act, I don't think the emotions are ever supposed to stop. No matter how many times you've had to pull the trigger and take someone's life.

"Squirters! Multiple targets in the open, twelve o'clock, one hundred and fifty meters!" Gonzalez reported over the radio and loud enough so that I could hear and was aware of what he saw.

However, my team leader didn't have to. Before Gonzalez could speak, my eyes had already locked onto the squirters exiting the building. *Shit!* I thought to myself. *That sure looks a hell of a lot more than the two guys from our intel.*

"I don't have a shot, Sgt!" I shouted to Gonzalez, who was now aiming at the targets. The laser from his M4 shone a bright, glowing dot on the backs of one of the squirters. He neither could engage as the chasing squad was in close proximity to the squirters. The wasn't a visible threat of any weapons either. Despite encountering fierce resistance, we could not fire, even with the lax rules of engagement that came with being in a special operations unit.

It turned out that the intelligence from the TOC was not only inaccurate but was so, by a large degree. There were ten enemy combatants on the objective instead of two or three bad guys. The enemy must have known that they were potentially being watched. So, they only allowed two men to leave the building at any given time.

Their strategy, leaving in pairs, was a tactic that we hadn't encountered before. Moreover, it displayed how knowledgeable our enemy was of our tactics. After seeing thousands of their comrades die in combat, it was only a matter of time before they eventually had a stroke of tactical genius.

As second squad followed, shots from their M4 suppressed rifles rang out, striking one of the squirters. I could see, from my position, as the target fell face-first into the dirt. His momentum caused his body to tumble like ragweed before coming to a stop. Second squad was close enough to the enemy to see that they were armed. However, for whatever reason, the enemy found it unnecessary to shoot.

"One target down." A voice from one of the members of second squad sounded over our radios. It was our platoon medic who put a few rounds into the target. A rarity that Doc was able to engage the enemy in combat. He could make it his entire career and never have to fire a shot. The medics' main purpose was to preserve life and not take it. But that's what made being a Ranger so unique. You may be called to step up to the plate, whether it's in your job description or not.

As the foot pursuit continued, Doc and one of the assaulters from second squad stayed back with the enemy he had shot. They didn't want to pass up the body and have the risk that he may still be alive, able to engage our guys once they ran by. It was a good thing that they decided to do so. The downed enemy fighter was still alive with multiple bullet holes in his body. Due to the laws of the Geneva convention, our medic had to render him aid.

The squirters continued to run, carrying AK-47 rifles while some had them strapped to their backs. They were in a dead sprint, heading towards a large depression in the terrain.

"Frag out!" Cortez shouted, indicating that he was in the process of throwing one of his M67 fragmentation grenades. Each Ranger on the assault team carried anywhere from one to three, sometimes more, depending on the operation. Rarely did they have to use them. Instead, shooting the enemy at close range was usually the preferred killing method. It also lessened the likelihood of injuring non-combatants and friendly forces.

Seconds later, the sound of the grenade detonating echoed throughout the night air. A thick cloud of dust rose skyward, void of the apocalyptic fireball depicted in Hollywood films. Faint whispers of shrapnel cut through the atmosphere, causing me to flinch and lower my head.

"Grenade!" An assaulter from second squad shouted. Members of second squad took a few steps back before falling belly first on the ground.

One of the squirters, hiding in sparse shrubs in the depression, tossed a grenade at the assaulting team. Simultaneously, a few of the enemy began blindly firing their AK47s. Luckily, the grenade fell short and exploded harmlessly in the field. The enemy gunfire sounding like metal snaps in the air from the bullets moving faster than the speed of sound was far from endangering Cortez and his men. However, knowing that the enemy had grenades in their possession only worsened the situation. Although, it would be a short-lived one.

Moments after the enemy grenade detonated, the assaulting team was back on their feet and began engaging the enemy. Only this time, with a level of violence put on full display, I had yet to see. Each man on the assaulting team returned fire and lobbed grenades back at the enemy. The loud barrage of bullets and grenades, all at once, was akin to what I'd only heard in movies. The audible sound of destruction and devastation, for a moment, seemed impossible for only a few men to produce.

Then, silence. As quickly as second squad engaged the enemy, it ended. Initially, I expected to hear blood-curdling screams and moans from the enemy. A sound that I had become familiar with during that deployment. Unusual noises a man makes after his limbs have been torn from his body after an explosion before expiring. But, instead, there was nothing. There was only a smoke-filled scene, with the fresh smell of gunfire in the air as the assaulters observed where the enemy was.

"Multiple EKIA. The second squad is good to go up on all equipment and personnel. We'll need a moment to sort the bodies out, determine how many to be exact, and search them for any intel." Cortez stated, talking to the ground force commander.

"Negative." Our commander replied without hesitation. "Fuck em.' We'll look at the overhead footage once we're back at base. In the meantime, let's get things sorted out inside the building and grab any intel we can inside. Besides, we have one that's still alive near the objective that Doc is currently working on. So, we can question him if he has anything and go from there. Roger?"

"Roger that," Cortez replied with a sense of relief in the tone of his voice. I could only imagine not having to sort through the soup of bodies was a huge satisfaction. While I could not see the destruction inside the depression, I could imagine what it must have looked like. There were upwards of eight or nine grenades that erupted, and hundreds of 5.56 rounds fired in a short amount of time. Each enemy fighter had been well serviced, with little left behind to investigate. It would have been like trying to put multiple Humpty Dumpty's back together again. And none of us on the ground that night wanted any parts of that task.

Doc Leo had already gathered valuable information back where the downed fighter was.

"This guy is only a teen! Freaking fourteen years old, out here fighting us. Fourteen!" A stunned Doc Leo announced. Individually, we all felt some kind of way. After learning that one of the fighters we were engaging wasn't even old enough to hold a driver's license had he been in the United States. I had to take a moment to realize exactly how young fourteen actually was. At that age, I was in middle school. A time in my life that I consider to be some of the most adventurous and fun. There wasn't a point that I could ever imagine engaging in combat. And I'm sure there was a moment of putting things into perspective for all of us. Seeing how good we had it. How different our lives could have been if it weren't because we were born in one of the greatest countries on earth. It was also a moment of realization for me. From then on, I understood that the enemy we faced weren't always middle-aged men. Some could very well be much younger than I was. A child.

After the assault team killed the squirters and gathered what they could from the target building, we were soon on our flight back to base. We left the bodies where they were. The depression they attempted to take shelter from within became their final resting place. I'm sure that tonight's mission will remain with me until my last living breath. It was one of the most traumatizing events that I've experienced. I can only be thankful that we could all make it out in one piece.

ATROPINE

Atropine. Well, that's what tends to stick out the most in my mind when I'm reminded of a particular mission while deployed to Iraq. Not the operational code name itself or the location of where it all took place. Instead, what first comes to mind, is a prescription medicine used as an involuntary nervous system blocker. During the first few weeks of basic infantry training in the Army, there is a brief instructional period on Atropine given to new recruits. However, the lessons were quick due to the unlikelihood that you would ever have to use them.

Ironically, my first introduction to this involuntary nervous system blocker wasn't in a military classroom. Instead, I first saw its use as a child, sitting on my living room floor. My dad and I were watching what would become one of my favorite movies, The Rock, starring Nicholas Cage. Cage, an FBI chemical warfare expert, searches for VX nerve gas in the film. A highly toxic synthetic chemical agent developed for the military and used in chemical warfare operations. However, the toxin was being held by a group of rogue Force Recon Marines at the notorious Alcatraz prison, threatening to use it on American soil. While searching for the weapons, Cage comes in contact with the gas and is poisoned. Shortly thereafter, he then begins to convulse and lose the function of his muscles.

However, because of his training and background in chemical warfare, Cage knew the only way to save himself was to inject Atropine. So, in the movie, he injects it directly into his chest, aiming for his heart before the VX gas's effects eventually kill him. And as dramatic of a scene, it was, watching the lead character stab himself in his heart, Hollywood's depiction of how to administer the medicine wasn't too far off. Besides how one would administer a life-saving dose of Atropine, the scenario in which to do so was pretty spot on.

From what I can recall, the Atropine shot given to our armed forces comes in two cylindrical syringes with a thin needle at the tip. The idea was to inject oneself directly into a muscle at the onset of chemical poisoning. As instructed by our medics, the muscle of choice was in the upper thigh or the upper buttocks region. Administering the shot was a lot similar to the EpiPen. Auto injected and pre-filled to a prescribed dose.

According to the medics in basic training, we had a fairly short window of time to inject ourselves with Atropine in the case of a chemical attack. Once injected, the effects of the drug should allow us the time needed to survive and seek further medical treatment. However, the emphasis on the likelihood of needing Atropine felt like our instructors were simply checking the box. After all, by the time I entered basic training, the war in Iraq was already a couple of years underway. The threat of a chemical attack seemed to have faded once American troops were on the ground. Instead, threats from roadside bombs and the lack of uniforms from the enemy opposition became a greater threat at that time.

For those of you who do not recall, before the war in Iraq officially kicked off in 2003, there was a lot of talk regarding the nation's ability to conduct a chemical attack. One of the reasons for invading was that military strategists believed Saddam Hussein owned chemical weapons stockpiles. These godforsaken weapons were known as WMD, weapons of mass destruction. And the best defense in preventing a WMD attack, at home or abroad, was to have a greater offense and hit them first. In July of 2003, American forces did just that.

However, the threat of a WMD attack was far less of a concern when I joined the Army. Quite honestly, the thought of having to fight against it never crossed my mind. And judging by the instructional period we received on chemical warfare in basic, I wasn't the only one who felt this way. But if being in the military had taught me a valuable lesson, it was to always apply Murphy's Law. The law states that "anything that can go wrong can and will go wrong."

I, and the Rangers on operation Simpson, would soon be faced with the threat of WMD. We were tasked to conduct yet another high-stakes mission on that same night. After wrapping up that mission, we found intelligence on the objective that would lead us to a new target a few miles away. This new target potentially contained highly sought-after WMD. According to the intel, the foreign fighters we killed were in charge of producing and disseminating these weapons. The WMD would later be employed throughout the battlefield against allied forces.

It was the first time that I had heard the term, weapons of mass destruction, used since my time in the country. At first, many of us were confused and found the information hard to believe. After all these years of scouring the country, we finally found what so many had been searching for. Since invading the country, in 2003, hundreds of thousands of US and allied forces had been on the lookout for such weapons, only to come up empty-handed.

During my first few weeks in Iraq, keeping our NBC (nuclear biological and chemical) suits close by was considered standard operating procedure. At times, bringing our gas masks on missions was normal practice if chemical weapons were used against us. However, after thousands of operations, we finally decided against carrying all of our NBC suits and gear into combat. Although, we always made sure that it was on our packing list. Deciding to keep it tucked away in our deployment bags or underneath our beds back at the base instead.

Follow-on missions were something that we learned to adjust to quickly. Especially during our Iraq deployment to the city of Tikrit. A follow-on was a mission we would conduct immediately after a raid. For example, we would find valuable information on the target during the initial operation. That information would then lead us to another target. These follow-on operations could sometimes run up to two or three missions in one night, depending on the intel.

Follow-on operations often took a toll on our bodies. However, they were some of the most exciting. And as a new guy on the team, they were where I learned and gained the most experience. The planning process for these operations was often on the fly and left little to no time for a formal planning process. As a result, we lacked the overhead imagery that we would typically get back at the TOC and an extensive dossier on the targets that we were after.

The planning was usually conducted immediately after the initial raid or flying in a

Blackhawk helicopter. And in most cases, planning for a follow-on would take place in a matter of a few minutes. First, planning would be carried out by the ground force commander and squad leaders, then trickled down to the team leaders. From there, the team leaders would inform each man on their team and what would be needed of them to have a successful operation.

While the planning was brief, it was what we trained for. Being a Ranger meant taking on some of the most challenging tasks. In theory, you could put a Ranger in the middle of a warzone, and he would come out victorious. Regardless of their equipment or the knowledge they had regarding their enemy. The most valuable piece of equipment was the mentality of the Ranger. The willpower to complete any task at hand, even if it meant doing it with his hands tied behind his back. Something that has been beaten into him since his training began.

Most of the follow-ons we conducted were nothing more than a standard raid. Our bread and butter. Something that we became masters of during the global war on terrorism. Raid operations were what we trained for, day in and day out stateside, before deploying. In the past, prior to 9/11, Rangers were often reserved for security operations. If you're familiar with the film Black Hawk Down, the Rangers were the forces that secured the perimeter of an objective. A more elite special operations unit, such as the notorious Delta Force, were the ones that entered the building, conducting the raid. However, the Rangers took on these high-risk operations in Iraq and Afghanistan in present times. Thus, freeing up the payload for Delta force and specialized units alike.

After the Simpson raid, instead of planning while in flight, we staged and prepped for our follow-on in an aircraft hangar outside Balad, Iraq. Balad was a city north of Iraq's capital, Baghdad, and south of our home base, Tikrit. It was the closest base to where the WMD was located. And during our 2006 deployment, Balad was the site of sectarian violence between Sunni and Shi'ite militias.

The hangar was sparsely occupied by American and allied forces, with little activity around. It was located at the rear of an airfield in the middle of the desert, surrounded by open desert terrain on all four sides. On any given day, the hangar was mostly used by conventional soldiers. They used it to stage and launch missions during the day and as a location to refuel their aircraft that were enroute to outlying cities. The large hangar was one of the most spacious I had seen. It had everything you could imagine or need to prepare for any operation.

The hangar resembled a medium-sized, one-story building with no rooms or walls to divide the space. The ceiling rose upwards of forty feet, with large steel beams stretched across to hold it upright. Its exterior, a thin sheet of metal, and its front side exposed and open, large enough to fit an aircraft through. Pallets and crates of ammunition, neatly stacked inside, one on top of the other on the concrete floor. As well as enough food and water to properly outfit a force that quadrupled us in size.

While it lacked the amenities of a TOC, it was far better than being crammed inside the helicopter's interior.

"Alright, men! Listen up and gather around." The ground force commander shouted, standing in the center of the hangar. The sound of his voice reverberated and echoed against the walls, like inside the halls of a cathedral. He held a sheet of paper with handwritten notes and a sketch of a building in his hands.

Most of us were busy stocking up on ammunition, fresh batteries for our night vision goggles, and resupplying on water. First and second squads passed around a running water hose at the hangar's entrance. They were trying their best to rinse dried blood from their equipment and uniforms. An image I'll never forget. After such a hellacious battle, most of the guys on the assault teams, for a moment, shared the enemy's blood.

"First off, good shit out there tonight. I know a lot was going on, and things didn't go as we had initially planned. However, despite all of that, you kept your wits about you and didn't allow the enemy to throw us off of our game. So, I don't want any of that to go unnoticed. Even down to the new guys out with us tonight, good shit." He continued, only this time, making sure to make eye contact with two other Rangers and me, who were also on their first deployment. "And Second squad, I want you all to make sure you check in with the Doc and get your shit sorted out before we head back out. I know you took the brunt of the fight, and I'm glad you all have made it out in one piece, but we're going to need you again tonight. So, make sure that you tend to whatever cuts, bruises, or burns that need to be taken care of immediately following this briefing."

Although second squad was unshaken after their head-on encounter with the suicide bomber, our commander wanted to be certain. After the adrenaline from an intense combat operation wears off, you'd be surprised at the kinds of injuries that initially go unnoticed. I heard a few stories of guys being shot and not knowing about it until hours later. So, getting a second and third look from the Doc was in second squad's best interest.

"From what we've gathered from OP Simpson, we can expect the building to be much larger. About five times as much. We believe it is a warehouse that either serves as a storage facility or where WMD is manufactured. I've talked to the folks back at the TOC, and we should have eyes from above before our arrival. And, instead of hitting this target with one main assault squad, we'll be going in with all three teams. As for our security, the machine gun teams will provide us with that, making sure no one leaves or exits the objective. Due to the nature of the target, the only change up with the security teams is that I'll need them further away than I would typically like to have them. So, if there is any shooting, I want the machine gunners to make sure they have good sectors of fire. Only engage what you can comfortably and accurately engage after properly identifying their targets." The commander continued, except with a seriousness unlike one I had heard or seen during the deployment.

I knew the gravity of the mission, especially considering it had the potential of involving WMD. Although, the tone that our Commander had during the brief was something with which I was unfamiliar. We've been on countless high-risk operations with him during this deployment. He's been doing this since the war campaign began in 2001. In fact, rumor has it that he had one of the first kills in Iraq before he made it to the position of ground force commander. So, stepping into the unknown was something that I imagined he would be comfortable with.

Honestly, hearing him sound so concerned rubbed off on me a bit. I can't speak on behalf of the other Rangers, but I was nervous about our follow-on mission so far. It was like some kind of osmosis or something. The slight tremble in our commander's throat as he spoke spread into my state of consciousness. It was the first time that I could say I was sincerely terrified. However, being a new guy amongst seasoned warriors, I tried my hardest not to allow my emotions to manifest into an expression on my face.

I panned my eyes to the left and right, scanning the hangar to look at the Rangers around me. They each shared the same singular emotion on their faces to a man. A communal copy and paste expression of *screw it*! I tried to mimic them the best I could and force myself to display my best war face. But if this were a game of poker, my team leader, Gonzalez, could call my bluff on every hand dealt.

"Dude, we're all good. Take a breath and listen. The rest of the guys out here, and I have your back. So, I need you to have ours. Roger?" Gonzalez leaned over to me and whispered into my ear. He didn't want to attract the commander's attention, who was still giving his brief.

"Roger," I replied, nodding my head up and down.

That's the type of leader Gonzalez is known for. He had a disregard for his own personal well-being and state of mind in the interest of those he led into combat. Of course, he could be hard on the guys he looked after at times, and at times, a little too harsh. But at the end of the day, we knew that he genuinely cared. Regardless of how many push-ups he'd make his guys do for failing to perfect a given task. We understood that his approach was so that we could reach our full potential. He wouldn't want anyone on his team if they weren't always giving one-hundred and ten percent.

The few words that Gonzalez managed to whisper to me were all that I needed to hear at that moment. Being as young as I was at the time, an eighteen-year-old kid, I managed to pull myself out of my own head. Even if it were only for that split second, I could look at the bigger picture and the mission ahead of us. Sure, I was still a little scared of what could happen. However, this operation was greater than how I was feeling. Besides, I'm sure we were all a little hesitant deep down inside.

"Doc! You can start handing out doses of Atropine to the men. Each will receive a single dose of the medicine, while the team leaders will receive two. I know you've been a busy man tonight, Doc. Hell, we all have, but I hope we won't need your assistance for understandable reasons. You'll be with me, attached at the hip while we're on target if things decide to go south. And once you're finished passing out the Atropine, Doc, I need you front and center to give all of us a quick refresher on when and how to administer." The commander spoke, continuing the mission brief.

Is he serious? I said quietly to myself. As I would have never uttered the words aloud. I hadn't heard of or seen Atropine since my time in basic training. Even then, the Atropine that we used was for training purposes only. The syringes were empty, void of any sharp needled tips, and had gunk built on after years of being circulated through hundreds of basic training classes.

"It's been some time for all of us since we've last had instruction on it, so make sure you fuckers are listening up. It could save your life or the lives of others. Tonight, Atropine will be one of the most important components of your gear, next to your rifle." As the commander paused again, the hangar's interior fell perfectly silent. You could hear a pin drop inside the hangar. "Does anyone have any questions, concerns, or gripes?"

"Do we know approximately how many personnel are in or located around the target building? If any?" One of the assaulters from third squad asked, jotting down a few notes in his waterproof notepad.

"Negative. As of this moment, we do not have any intel that indicates that there will be anyone on location. That doesn't mean, however, that there won't be. As we've just learned from our last hit, intel can change at any moment. So, expect that there will be personnel on target and some with the potential to engage us. If this is a WMD facility, I'd assume they would have someone out there to protect it." The commander responded.

Doc Leo slowly walked around to each man, carrying a beaten-up, brown cardboard box with medical symbols on the sides. Inside were the syringes of Atropine that each of us were to receive.

As he came over to me and handed me my dose, I couldn't help but notice how surreal of a situation we were in. It also struck me that my unit, potentially, could be the first credited with finding WMDs. This would be the biggest, most gratifying news that came out of Iraq since the capture of Saddam Hussein.

"Alright, gentlemen, boys, and girls," Doc semi-jokingly announced, now making his way up to the front of the platoon to give us a medical brief. One that would be like any other that we ever received.

"What you are all holding could be the difference between going home or taking a trip to the dark side of reality. This is Atropine." Reaching above his head, Doc held a handful of the injectors. "While on the objective, if any of you begin to feel your faces melting off, you will need to inject this into your upper buttocks." A few of the guys let out a chuckle, momentarily lightening the mood in the hangar. "It's an auto-injector, so there's no need for much thinking other than simply administering.

And, if you're still having a challenging time figuring out how to take the shot, the instructions are pictured on the side. Also, like the oxygen masks on an airplane, you will give yourself the shot before trying to help a buddy. I need you all to keep this in your medical kits, where I and someone from your team can easily access it." He continued.

Each Ranger kept their medical kit in the same location on their body. In our platoon, the standard operating procedure was to have our kits on the left side of our body armor, just above the hip. However, there was more to the reasoning behind this other than uniformity. Doing so allowed any one of us to locate the kit in high-stress situations or in complete darkness. Searching around for someone's equipment could cost you precious time. So, we alleviated the issue by not storing it in a place that someone or the Doc wasn't familiar with.

After Doc finished his brief, he held a small gathering in one of the corners of the hangar, demonstrating the administration of Atropine. As we stood around him, I remember thinking how much it had differed from the movie, The Rock, I saw as a kid. There wasn't a long needle that protruded from one end of a syringe full of thick, gel-like medicine. Nor did you have to stick it into your chest, closest to the heart. The drastic comparisons were the only thing that allowed me to chuckle inside since the briefings began. Even if it were only for a second. The Atropine shot was anything but complicated or as dramatic as Hollywood depicted. It was simple. If we were having a reaction to the chemical threat, we'd immediately inject the medicine as directed.

"Let's get it on, men, and line it up! We'll be taking the same birds in. The helos are inbound, and then, we're wheels up in ten minutes!" Our commander shouted, gathering up and putting back on his ballistic armor.

"You good to go, Irv? Make sure you got everything! All mission essential gear, fresh batteries, and Atropine. All the good shit." Gonzalez asked me.

I was standing near the group, watching Doc put on an impromptu medical clinic. I wanted to make sure that I didn't miss a beat. It was like I was a sponge that sat in the sun all day and had dried out. I wanted to soak up and hold as much information as possible before heading out.

By now, information from the TOC had finally made its way over to us. We also received a nice overhead view of the WMD building from one of the nearby drones. The building resembled a large high school or a factory building that you'd see in a downtown metropolitan area. Made of brick, with windows stretching along the sides of the first and second floors. It almost looked as if it wasn't supposed to be there.

The suspected WMD building was located along the outskirts of the town, Samarra. Samarra wasn't an area we'd feel uncomfortable working in. While on our deployment, we had been to the city of Samarra on more than a few occasions. Its located north of Baghdad and sits on the east bank of the Tigris River. On the few operations we had conducted in Samarra, the resistance we met ranged from minimal to a butt-puckering factor of *Oh Shit*!

Based on the intel we had and were currently getting from the TOC, we expected anything but a quiet operation. While there hadn't been any known hostiles that occupied the building, drone footage indicated recent foot and vehicle traffic. Although, there was no means of determining exactly how many individuals there were. We had to take the information we were given with a grain of salt.

"Birds inbound, ladies!" The commander announced, giving us our last warning. If there were any last-minute changes that we needed to make, grab extra ammo, or take a piss, the time was now.

I could hear the propellers of our Blackhawks, steadily approaching, just outside the hangar. And while the audible sound of the helos flying in was something I was familiar with, the tone of the operation was almost unrecognizable. It was the first time that I took a personal pause to myself. I wanted to reflect on what led me to this point and everything we had already accomplished. This operation was one every soldier dreamed of being a part of.

I imagined what it would mean for all allied forces fighting in the country since the invasion. And what it would mean to everyone back home in the states, finally finding the elusive weapons of mass destruction. Finding these weapons represented everything we had sacrificed over the years and that our losses wouldn't be in vain. To be a part of an operation of this magnitude was what I dreamed it would be like, as a kid, being a member of a special operations unit.

The birds had finally landed, and we began filling on. Seated in the same arrangements as before. Gonzalez, to my side with our legs hanging from the side of the aircraft. The flight to Samarra was short from the Balad hangar compared to flying from our base in Tikrit. Less than forty miles total distance. Once we took off, a short twenty-minute flight time to wheels down on target.

The code name for this mission was dubbed

operation Phoenix. A term derived from a bird in ancient Greek and Egyptian mythology. It's believed that the bird would rise from its ashes, reborn again after burning. Although, unlike the phoenix, it was in our best interest that none of us would have to partake in life's death process. But if the gods of war determined that death was in our deck of cards that night, we would be born again.

How we'd take control of the objective would nearly mirror operation Simpson. The helos were going to land as closely as they could to the building. Again, to catch the enemy off-guard. Hopefully, while they were still asleep. My machinegun team, along with another, would secure the outer perimeter and minimize traffic to and from the building. The only difference is that the three assault squads, first, second, and third, would simultaneously enter and conduct the raid. Each team would then systematically and carefully clear the building of any threats.

Once the target was secured, both inside and its perimeter, only then would we begin the search for locating the WMD. If the assault teams were to come into contact with what we believed to be WMD, they would immediately notify the ground force commander after documenting and photographing the evidence. The commander would then inform the TOC, passing the intel up the chain of command. Then, military personnel more specialized in dealing with chemical weapons would then be called in to properly secure and dispose of them. Once the WMD was confirmed and destroyed, our mission would be deemed successful.

As with most of our flights with the 1/60th Night Stalkers, this was also uneventful. And that's how I'm sure we all appreciated them to be. It allowed us to keep our minds laser-focused on the mission before us. The only distinction between this flight, and the countless others, was the smell that permeated the air as we neared closer to the location of our target. A mixture of human feces, rotting garbage, and an aroma of stagnant water, reminiscent of the swamps at Ft. Benning Georgia back home. The feces and trash were something I expected and was used to in Iraq. While the origins of the aromatic fragrance of swamp water must have come from the Tigris.

"One minute!" Everyone shouted from within the Black Hawk.

We were quickly closing in on the objective. Large palm trees and what appeared to be small sand dunes scattered the terrain a few hundred feet beneath me. My arm hairs stood on end, and my heart throbbed inside my chest, smacking the center of my sternum like a pinball machine. Although a burst of adrenaline coursed throughout my veins on every mission, this rush was like none other.

Moments before landing, I decided to say a quick prayer to my God above. Silently asking for the protection of myself and my Ranger brothers around me. If anything were to happen, I at least wanted my last moments to have been in prayer. A practice that I strangely neglected in previous operations.

"Go! Go! Go!" Gonzalez shouted at the top of his lungs while simultaneously smacking me on my shoulder.

The bottom of my combat boots touched the hard Iraqi surface. Small rocks and fine gravel kicked up into the air from the helos chopping blades. For a moment, temporarily blinded me as I offloaded and tried to gain a visual of the suspected WMD facility. The assaulters must have had better visibility than I did on the landing. At a full sprint, I could see the silhouettes of their bodies running away from me and watched as they melted into the night. Their infrared lasers mounted on their rifles shined bright, bobbing up and down like lightsabers in front of them.

"Let's move, Irv! Buildings up ahead!" Gonzalez yelled from behind me. His voice overcame the loud sound of the Black Hawk's engines as they quickly took off into the dark sky.

Whatever pre-mission jitters I had back at the hangar and during the flight over seemingly evaporated. I was officially in a state of being, simply known as "The zone." It was the perfect mental state a soldier needs to be in to get the job done. Nothing else mattered at the moment. Not even myself. There were only two things that existed in this hypnotic-like state, the mission and the team of Rangers that were around me.

The scene looked like something you would expect out of a movie. After the dust had settled, I could finally see the target building. We landed less than two hundred yards from the building, and a lone building stood eerily in the distance. A few perfectly placed palm trees surrounded its eerie appearance and sparse vegetation that grew like weeds in open terrain.

The appearance of the building, at first, struck me as odd. I remember thinking how much it had differed from the grainy overhead pictures we had a chance to see back at the hangar. It was much larger and came nothing close to where I'd expect weapons of mass destruction to be stored. Some of the windows along its side were shattered and broken out. The building didn't appear to be occupied and abandoned for some time. And its exterior looked as if it had already seen its fair share of combat.

As the assault teams advanced towards the building, Gonzalez and I set up our machinegun on a small sand berm about a hundred yards away. The position was perfect for overlooking the building and providing security for the teams. From here, I was also able to make out a few homes and structures in the distance. Although, the outlying buildings didn't pose much of an immediate threat. Due to their distance from the objective, half a kilometer away, I wouldn't have to pay much attention to them.

"Breacher's up! Keep an eye out for squirters as the teams make their way in. Be sure to call out any targets as you see them, and I'll inform the guys." Gonzalez stated with his back facing against me. He kept a keen eye out for any threats that could sneak up behind us.

The muffled sound of a ballistic breach from a twelve-gauge shotgun reverberated into the night. Rather than use an explosive charge to gain entry, the team opted for something less likely to lead to a secondary explosion. Using a shotgun with ammunition specially designed to defeat the locks on a door was instead the assaults team's best option. Seconds after, I could hear the shouts of the assault teams, barking commands in Arabic, as they entered the building.

I watched the assault teams make their way through the large structure and clear it. My body was slightly tense and on high alert as I anticipated the worse. After operation Simpson, I was skeptical of the lack of chaos thus far on the objective. Unlike Simpson, which opened with a bang, this objective was anything but. Instead, it was strangely quiet and far from anything I had mentally prepared for.

Thankfully, there hadn't been any resistance, and the teams were wrapping up their clearing process. Thirty minutes had elapsed from the time that we landed until now. That's when the call that we anxiously waited for came over the radios,

"Jackpot. I repeat, we have a Jackpot. Beginning SSE time now." First squads squad leader calmly announced.

The *jackpot* was a reference the assault teams used on the target. It indicated that they had successfully secured what they were searching for. SSE was the acronym used for the sensitive site exploitation they conducted once an objective was properly cleared for potential threats. SSE was the assaulting squads ' bread and butter. That was, of course, next to room clearing and killing bad guys at close range.

"Damn, that was fast. Looks like they found the WMD. Keep an eye out, but we will be ex-filing out of here soon." Gonzalez said to me. I could hear the excitement in his voice, despite trying to maintain a sense of calmness and professionalism.

The nights' operation went as smooth and without incident as one could hope for. However, there was a slight issue regarding the WMD that the teams found inside the building. In fact, the weapons of mass destruction were anything but.

While what they discovered inside could technically be considered chemical weapons, they lacked the hype. Or at least what we had expected. And, in many ways, fell short of what we anticipated after years of the WMD build-up before the invasion.

"Yeah, we're not too sure what or who we'll be needing to come out here. All we have here is a bunch of chlorine. It's definitely a lot of it. Our guess is that it could be anywhere from a few hundred to a thousand gallons. But no evidence of anything else. So, we'll grab what we can and begin making our way out to exfil." First squads team leader announced over the radio.

"Dude, fucking chlorine? Did we just come out here with Atropine for some fucking chlorine? I guess." Gonzalez grunted under his breath but loud enough for me to hear.

I couldn't help but feel the frustration he felt. Hell, I'm sure most of us shared the same sentiment, if not all of us. We'd spent the last few hours preparing ourselves for what could have been one of the greatest finds during the war. In my mind, I went over and over again countless potentials and what-ifs. I thought about death and what my last moments would have been like, succumbing to chemical poising. Or, God forbid, the enemy putting up their last hoorah, in defense of the weapons they took care of in hiding all these years. As well as what it would mean to everyone back home making a discovery of this magnitude.

Unlike the Nicholas Cage movie, this operation was anything far from sharing a dramatic ending. F-16 fighter jets wouldn't fly overhead as I held flares into the sky, signaling mission accomplished. And thankfully, none of us would have to make the conscious decision to inject ourselves with Atropine before our faces melted and our bodies convulsed on the ground. As far as I was concerned, the Atropine injectors would have been better off if they were left back at the hangar. Having it on me gave me the same vibes I would get when carrying a live grenade. I absolutely hated it. While it is a life-saving device, if not taken care of or used correctly, it could cause more harm to yourself than good.

After the teams took pictures and gathered the little intelligence they could, our 1/60th was back in the air to pick us up. However, our commander decided that we would destroy the building and the contents inside. Shortly after the Iraq campaign began, a few reports indicated that enemy fighters were looking to weaponize the chemical in their operations. Al Qaeda wanted to inflict as much death and destruction as possible. Using chlorine, in combination with their most effective tactics, was what they had in mind.

The idea was that they could detonate a vehicle with makeshift explosives and chlorine to produce a crude chemical weapon. Far from the chemicals we were accustomed to hearing, such as Anthrax or mustard gas. However, the makeshift WMD would have adverse side effects on those nearby if one were detonated.

After operation Phoenix and the destruction of the chlorine, we saw the first use of these chemical bombs. Later that year, in October, we learned of Al Qaeda conducting attacks in the city of Ramadi using the chemical. A vehicle loaded with mortars and chlorine tanks exploded, injuring four people, civilians and three Iraqi police. While not as effective as the enemy had hoped, the attacks continued throughout that year and into 2007. While people were sickened from the chlorine attacks, it was reported that no one died due to chemical poisoning. The casualties that unfortunately did occur were instead from the explosions.

While operation Phoenix was far from anything we planned for, it was still a success at the end of the day. Hell, any mission that we can all walk away alive from was great. Being a new guy and getting used to the work we did every night mattered the most. It wasn't about how many bad guys we killed or captured on target. Mission success was all about making sure you and the guys made it back home safe. And in this case, the icing on the cake was denying the enemy a chance to use the chlorine we discovered in potential future attacks.

That's how war is, I suppose. You were never sure what you may or may not encounter on the battlefield. Or how far the impact of a mission may reverberate long after the dust has settled. At times, it can be absolute hell on earth, and at others, the greatest enemy you're fighting is your own mind and complete boredom. One minute, you're watching the guys around you get blown up by a suicide bomber. Then, the next, you're taking pictures of chlorine in an empty storage facility.

That's what I found to love the most about the career I fought tooth and nail for and was so grateful to be a part of. Regardless of all the terrifying things that could happen on the battlefield, everyone was more than willing to walk down that valley of death beside you. As I was, as well with them. Personal fear was something we all learned to shove away and stuff into our back pockets. What mattered the most was having each one another's backs and making sure that we all made it home to see our families. For that, I will forever be thankful.

MOLDED FOR WAR

Tonight, was a lot like the previous nights in Marjah. In fact, it was no different. We walk a few hundred meters, defend against an ambush, and the cycle continues and repeats. Walk, shoot a few bad guys, and walk some more. The pattern of violence continued from the moment we were dropped off via Chinook helicopter and continued to the objective. The fighting only ceased during our exfil, and we loaded back up in the helo. If we were lucky.

That was the tone of our 2009 deployment,

conducting operations in the small city of Afghanistan. During its peak, my unit was there, and Marjah was the Wild Wild West. Our rotation for this deployment happened to be during the summer. A season when the Taliban seemed to enjoy fighting us the most, instead of the cold winters.

    I guess I can't blame the enemy for that. No matter how much I despised them. The Taliban, wanting to come out and play in the heat, was one of the few smartest battlefield decisions they could have made. Afghanistan during the winter months was absolutely brutal. A cold that was so frigid, it felt like your skin was being cut with a thousand razors. With every breath of the wind, your bones felt like they were being pinched in vice grips.

    I absolutely hated fighting in the winter. Everything you touched felt as cold as ice. The tips of my fingers went numb, holding my SR-25 sniper rifle after a few minutes. Making shooting in harsh and extreme conditions that much more of a challenge. Luckily, the main challenge I faced during this deployment was prioritizing which targets to shoot first. However, in the summer of 2009, there were plenty of enemy threats and bad guys to engage. The fighting became so intense that it felt like we were fighting a small-sized army.

Marjah is in southern Afghanistan, located in Helman Provence. A small city much less densely populated than cities such as Kabul and Kandahar. During our deployment in 2009, Marjah was known to be a safe haven for Taliban fighters. At this same time, our British allies suffered more than one hundred casualties in the city. Marjah was the place to be if you wanted to get in on the action and earn your tax-free combat pay. All one hundred and fifty bucks of it.

We had one main goal that we were tasked to accomplish during our four-month deployment. Eliminate as much of the Taliban presence as possible. Unannounced to us, President Obama was gearing up to send thousands of Marines to Marjah after our deployment ended. Our job was to destroy and disrupt the Taliban in the area before the Marines arrived. It was a perfect task for Charlie company, first platoon, and something they became proficient in over the years.

I was serving as the platoon sniper for Charlie companies, first platoon. In terms of battalion, that's the platoon where I was born. Since stepping foot in the 3rd Ranger Battalion, Charlie Company, first platoon had been the only platoon I served in. That's where my career began, after serving as a machine gunner, team leader, assaulter, etc. I was fortunate enough that I would be deploying with my old company again. While serving as a sniper, the platoon we would eventually work with was never set in stone. So, after moving to the sniper platoon at headquarters, getting the opportunity to reconnect with old teammates was a blessing in more ways than one.

We had been in country for a couple of months now, and we were in our groove. We had our gear and equipment figured out and knew what worked and didn't. My weapon of choice was none other than my suppressed SR-25, which I made sure to keep a fresh coat of camouflaged spray paint on. I even chose to give her a nickname, Dirty Diana. A song inspired by the late Michael Jackson, who surprisingly passed during this deployment.

The SR-25 is a semi-automatic sniper rifle that fired a 7.62 mm projectile. And fitted on the top of her was a ten-powered Leopold scope, along with night vision optics. I was particular with this weapon because it could fire multiple shots in rapid succession. Unlike what most people imagine when thinking of a sniper rifle or have seen in a film. A bolt action, precision weapon, similar to most hunting rifles. They operate manually, where the shooter ejects each round and loads another after each shot.

I carried no less than two hundred rounds on me on about every operation in Helmand. It was a standard loadout regarding the amount of ammo I'd take. Although, there were a few instances that I thought it was far too small of an amount. Some nights after a mission, I would return to my room on the base with a magazine of twenty rounds or less.

Due to the intensity of the firefights, most of the bullets I fired were only meant to keep the enemy at bay. While other shots were one hundred percent intended to kill bad guys. And by this point in our deployment, I already had a couple of dozen kills under my belt. And tonight's operation, there was a high probability that the number of enemy combatants I killed would rise.

Tonight's mission was simple and one that we were accustomed to. Kill, or capture an enemy high-value target who operated and coordinated attacks within Marjah. Killing him, being our most preferred approach if the opportunity presents itself. The target we were after was believed to be the maker and facilitator of IEDs in the area. Some were previously used to kill soldiers in the prior weeks and months.

We pinned his location to a building deep in the heart of Marjah. It was believed that he kept a shield of protection around him. Going as far as using the locals living in his vicinity as his muscle and security. While it wasn't unheard of for the Taliban to use the local population, he maintained an unusual amount of them. So, while we were used to fighting whenever we worked in the city, we expected a high probability of heavy resistance tonight.

We left our home base in Kandahar just after the sunset into the Afghan horizon. The dark skies above were peppered with beautiful stars, planets, and constellations. It reminded me of my childhood, visiting my grandparents in the country and gazing up into the heavens with my dad. He had a huge appreciation for astronomy, passing down his admiration for it to me at a very young age. However, growing up in an environment littered with artificial light made stargazing a challenging hobby. So, finally getting away from it all and under the country skies was an event we took advantage of.

It was also much cooler than usual. The thermometers that night read a comfortable eighty-five degrees. While those temperatures stateside are considered hot, in the desert, that was normal. Here, where one-hundred and twenty degrees during the day were expected, over a thirty-degree drop in temperature was appreciated. Working under the cover of darkness was one of the benefits of being a Ranger. Unlike conventional forces, who worked primarily under blistering hot temperatures during the day. Working at night also granted us the ability to accomplish more without the threat of heat exhaustion.

After receiving our brief back in Kandahar, we flew in on CH-47 Chinook helicopters, landing a few kilometers outside Marjah's outskirts. The CH-47 was rather large and considered one of the heaviest lifting aircraft in the US arsenal. Also operated by the 1/60th Night Stalkers, it was our preferred means of travel, especially in the Afghan mountainous terrain. A tandem-rotor helicopter, having two rotors instead of one, like the Blackhawk, with a top speed of one hundred and eighty-eight miles per hour.

Landing outside the city allowed us to get as

close as possible to our target without spooking him. A pair of Chinooks flying overhead was unmistakable and could be heard approaching from miles away. Especially on clear, quiet nights like tonight. Although, no matter how far we landed outside the city's limits, we were almost always greeted with the sounds of gunfire. Tonight, was no different.

The skyline over Marjah lit up like a Christmas tree with enemy tracers and gunfire upon landing. The enemy in the area used it as an early warning system. Any bad guys operating in the area, would quickly be alerted that American troops would soon be moving in. As rudimentary as their warning system seemed, it worked relatively well.

To kill or capture our target, we would have to move quickly. So, our best bet would be to try and avoid as much of the enemy resistance as possible. The last thing we wanted was to have an extended shootout leading up to the objective. But, if we were to engage the enemy, we would do so using extreme precision and violence. We were on somewhat of a timeline to reach our high-value target before he could escape.

"Head on a swivel, Mike, and keep an eye out on the rooftops. Call out any threats as you see them." I radioed my spotter over our sniper team's internal comms walking into the heart of Marjah. Mike was my spotter for most of this deployment before his injury a few weeks later. He was a few years older than I was and had some prior service time under his belt. Mike was previously in the Navy and served there for a brief stint before coming over to the better side of the armed forces. The Army.

Even though we butted heads on a few occasions, it was rare, and I could count them on one hand. Most of our friction came from Mike's strange struggle when hitting a three-hundred-meter target. Mike was able to hit a man-sized target ten football fields away. But, for unexplainable reasons, it was a hit or miss on an identical target, three football fields away. I didn't fault him for it, although I did find it a little odd.

Unlike my SR-25, a semi-automatic rifle, Mike carried a .300 Winchester Magnum. It's a bolt-action sniper rifle that fired an absolute beast of a projectile. The bullet had the same striking energy as a .357 magnum fired at point-blank range on a target a kilometer away. While Mike loved his precision rifle, I had a love and hate relationship with it. Although it was an extremely accurate weapon that packed one hell of a punch, it only held five rounds. Furthermore, because it was a bolt action, engaging targets as fast as I liked added difficulty I'd rather be without.

"Movers, twelve o'clock, two hundred meters. No weapons are present at this time." The squad leader of first squad announced over the radio for all of us to hear. His role throughout the deployment was to serve as the point man. The point man's task was planning out the routes we would take, leading us to the objective. If there were any obstacles or potential threats ahead of us, he usually was the first to lay eyes on them.

"Roger that, One-Charlie. Continue on, and

I'll send Sierra up ahead to provide us some overwatch." Our platoon sergeant, Munn, replied.

Sierra, short for sniper, was my sniper team's assigned designator used for radio dialog. Sergeant Munn made the battlefield decision to send my two-man element ahead of the platoon to keep an eye on the individuals. Mike and I had somewhat of a reputation as snipers providing overwatch for the platoon thus far. If the platoon ever contacted the enemy and a firefight ensued, it was usually over quickly.

With our night vision scopes, we could see what most of the guys in the platoon couldn't see. And coupled with my suppressor on the SR-25, my shots remained quiet. Not allowing my rifle firing to be heard over great distances.

"Let's move. I'll engage the first target with you on the follow-ups if we see any weapons." I whispered to Mike as we began making our way towards the front of the platoon.

We'd had a surprisingly good reputation in keeping the guys in the platoon safe. I wasn't going to lose that kind of a reputation anytime soon.

"Contact, six o'clock, eighty meters!" Sergeant Farr shouted aloud.

Machine-gun fire erupted before Mike, and I could get ahead of first squad. It sounded like it was coming from behind a few mud huts to our left. Green tracers flew feet above our heads, and their super-sonic snaps popped as they screamed by.

Everyone dropped to the ground to avoid getting hit and looked for a place to find some cover. Something sparse and hard to come by initially. The only available cover was determined by how much you could press your body against the ground and hope to not get hit. Our movement was along a narrow road that led throughout the city. Tactically, walking along pathways and streets was something that we tried to avoid. Since the roads in Marjah were ideal for Taliban IEDs and the perfect place to set up an ambush.

Staying as low as possible, Mike and I continued to press forward towards Sergeant Farr and his squad, who were now laying down heavy cover fire. The purpose of covering fire wasn't necessarily meant to kill the enemy. Instead, it was designed to disrupt their offensive assault and allow us to gain a strategical upper hand. Once we gained superiority through a barrage of gunfire, even if for a split second, we could accurately locate and eliminate the threat. And in combat, the difference between life and death is a matter of fractions of a second.

Arriving at Farr's location, I could determine where some gunfire was coming from. Like sparklers on the fourth of July, muzzle flashes flickered from behind the side of a building. Less than one hundred meters from my location, a lone shooter firing an AK-47 became visible. Although there was also fire coming from elsewhere, this target was my most immediate concern for the time being. Taking the AK-47 out of the fight would allow us to focus on the machinegun fire.

"Mike!" I shouted to Mike, lying close and off to my right side. We lie flat on our bellies, looking through our night vision scopes and focusing on the target. "Got one to my twelve. Give me a spot and follow up if I need one. He might have someone working with him, so drop him if somebody else pops out."

The chances of me missing a shot at a target less than a football field away were slim. Although, if I were to miss or have something happen to my rifle, I wanted Mike dialed in and ready to take the shot.

The enemy's bullets continued to snap and wiz overhead. Some landed dangerously close by, impacting the ground in front of and around, creating a *thud* sound as they hit. I can best describe the sound as if someone were punching a carpeted floor or a boxer beating a heavy bag. Muffled, but carried an intensity that you knew would be devastating if one were to hit you. A few struck dangerously close, causing the earth underneath us to vibrate.

"Sending!" I yelled, indicating to everyone that I was about to fire.

The crosshairs in my scope were dialed in and centered on the upper chest cavity of my target, crisp and still. My breathing was as calm and deliberate, despite the chaos around us. Being calm under these conditions was no easy task. Although, it was something that we trained for, for hours on end until the technique was perfected. The scenery around me no longer existed at that moment leading up to the shot. I was in a bubble of serene consciousness. Only myself, my rifle, and the target I was about to engage existed.

In unison with my breathing and weapon, I slowly yet deliberately took the slack out of my trigger. The slightest pressure would send my bullet on its final path and into my target. I no longer identified a human on the receiving end. He was simply a three-dimensional chunk of flesh and bone that stood between myself and those around me from making it home.

Crack!

I fired my SR-25, sending a 7.62 hollow-tip projectile traveling at two thousand six hundred feet per second towards my target. As I fired, the recoil from my rifle caused the individual firing his AK-47 to briefly disappear from inside my scope. I knew that everything leading up to the shot was perfect. My range was dialed in. I had no need to factor in the wind due to the short distance and lack of a breeze.

"Impact!" Less than a second elapsed after I fired before Mike shouted out that I did indeed hit my target.

I quickly regained focus on where the target was and prepared for a second shot. But I wouldn't need to send another. The enemy, firing from a semi-kneeling position, now lay motionless on his back. His upper body, where I placed my bullet, fell behind the edge of the building. Only his lower half and feet pointed skyward were exposed and slightly covered by a light-colored garment.

"One EKIA. Sierra is moving locations to get an eye on the remaining targets." I announced over my radio to Sgt. Munn, who was located towards the rear of our platoon.

The sounds of enemy machine-gun fire slowed slightly but remained effective and prevented our platoon's advance. Then, picking up my SR-25, Mike and I began making our way to a better position to view the battlefield. A few meters to the rear of where I had taken the shot, a small outlying hut would provide a good vantage point. The structure stood less than twenty feet in height. Resembling what your typical backyard tool shed would look like in the states. It would allow my sniper team to view the enemy's position by gaining access to its roof.

I told Mike that we would be doing a short climb and to prepare the telescopic ladder he carried on his back. As I began to set up the ladder and make my accent, I heard the voice of an assaulter squawk into my ear over my radio. "One EKIA. Sierra, you're going to have two targets moving to the East, about one-hundred meters."

"Roger that." I acknowledged.

I was happy to hear that the guys on the ground finally spotted where the fire was coming from. Our luck so far in Afghanistan, locating the enemy was challenging at times. The Taliban knew the terrain like the back of their hands and used it to their advantage. I thought fighting the Taliban was like fighting ghosts in a few instances.

The Taliban reminded me of the stories I read as a kid and soldiers fighting the Viet Cong guerrilla forces in Vietnam. An elusive enemy. One who seemingly popped out of thin air and opened fire on the troops from the thick jungle. Only to disappear in the same manner. The Taliban's fighting tactics and use of the environment around them were strikingly similar. It felt like mountains' sides and thick vegetation were opening fire on us during some engagements. Rarely seeing the enemy at all.

By now, two of the assault squads, second and third, began a flanking maneuver to try and cut off the fleeing Taliban fighters. Nevertheless, enemy fire at our platoon's position continued, although it was sporadic at best. After clearing the structure's rooftop, Mike and I established a good firing position and searched for the two remaining fighters.

"Mike, shine your floodlight over there, in that patch of foliage. That's where I'd be setting up if I were them." I stated.

Thick foliage stretched along a row of mud huts in the direction the assaulters suspected the targets to be heading. It was the only area that offered the fighters any type of concealment. I wanted Mike to use his infrared laser to illuminate the vegetation, hoping that I'd catch a glimpse of the enemy. And, having a background myself as a machine gunner, it would be a place I would employ my machine gun team.

Brraaatttt! A long, sustained burst from an RPK machine gun opened fire, sending the flanking assault teams to the ground. Green tracers flew through the air above the assaulters. Some of the rounds smacked surrounding huts and broke tree branches above them. The surrounding structures echoed the gunfire and sounded as if it came from a violent thunderstorm.

"Got 'em!" Mike and I shouted, in almost perfect unison, as the erupting enemy fire caught our eyes.

As I suspected, the Taliban had set up a hasty fighting position from within the foliage. Mike quickly focused on the targets, bathing them with his floodlight. The outline of two bodies immediately stood out to me. One of the men was lying on his stomach as he fired the weapon. The other, squatting close to his partner with a shiny AK-47 strapped to his back. As the fighter squatted, I watched as he shouted in Pashtu, which I assumed to be the command to fire.

My rifle was already sighted in, and I needed no permission to fire. I pasted the crosshairs of my scope onto the silhouette of the fighter behind the gun. Flashes of light from the barrel of the RPK lit up like bright camera flashes. I took up the little slack in my trigger and firmly pressed it back. *Snap*! Dirty Diana again sang her song of death.

Unlike my first shot, I maintained a sight picture of the target, fighting through the rifle's gentle recoil. His head jolted and snapped back as if the motion occurred three times normal speed. Then, a cloud of liquid exploded up and outward from his backside, and his body released all tension. The bullet struck him in the space between his head and shoulder, just above the clavicle. Immediately ending the life that he had in him.

"Impact," I announced over to Mike before he had a chance to do so.

"Second target is on the move. Give me a two mil lead and send it when ready." After eliminating the first enemy fighter, Mike gave me the information I needed to hit the remaining target.

A two mil lead was the distance he estimated I needed to hit the fighter, who was now on the move. Inside the scopes that we used, the reticles are referred to as MIL dot. Along the horizontal and vertical crosshairs are four small circles. Each circle/dot is a unit of measurement that a sniper and his spotter use to accurately engage targets. Factoring in the distance, speed, and angle the target moved away from our position, Mike knew how far ahead I needed to aim to hit the target. Thus, causing the fleeing Taliban fighter to run into my bullet as I fired. The math wasn't always exact in these conditions, and other factors came into play if given the time. However, it would get me close enough to make adjustments if needed.

After applying the lead Mike gave me, I steadied my crosshairs in front of the fighter as he ran. The AK-47 he had strapped on his back was now in his hands. The assaulters below began to engage the enemy, although none were successful in hitting him. I watched their smaller caliber rounds fired from their M4 rifles bounce and skip around him as they fired.

Damn! He sure can move with the clothes and shoes he has on. The thought silently made its way through my mind as I watched the man in loose-fitting garments and sandals sprinting. I was almost impressed that he could maneuver the way he was through such thick brush and the shifty gravel beneath his feet. Even more so, he was doing it at night.

"Sending," I mumbled, barely loud enough for Mike to hear as I let out the air in my lungs before taking the shot.

"Son of a bitch!" I hissed in frustration. Just as I broke the shot, the fighter changed direction, causing my round to miss off to his side.

Before I could get my second shot off, Mike's .300 unsuppressed Winchester Magnum let out a deafening *BANG*. The man I was fixated on suddenly tumbled forward and disappeared into the brush. It was like watching a human-sized tumbleweed as his momentum carried his body face-first into the earth. Mike's bullet hit him with such devastating force that the fighter was dead before hitting the ground.

"One Charlie, this is Sierra. Two enemy KIA, all clear. Over." I spoke into my radio, informing sergeant Munn that the remaining targets were eliminated.

"Good shooting Mike. That fucker must

have known I was about to end him, huh?"

"Yeah, roger that. I'm sure that's what happened." Mike said with a grin that spread from one side of his face to the other. "That's what I'm here for, Irv. Someone's gotta save your ass."

I didn't take Mike's joke to heart and even shared in on the laugh with him as we gathered our gear and made our way down to the platoon. However, missing the shot did affect me. While I knew I would miss a target from time to time, and it wasn't my first, it was something I would always beat myself up about later on. Missing the easy shots, as a sniper team leader, was something I wasn't allowed to do. Despite that, I was glad to have my spotter, who was always willing to pick up the ball whenever I dropped it.

After killing the Taliban fighters, a few assaulters searched their bodies. Gathering any intel they may have carried on them and destroyed their weapons. But the mission was far from over and had only begun. The high-value targets location was still a few kilometers from us, and we needed to make up some time. The firefight was less than a ten-minute encounter, but there would be more knowing the city of Marjah. Spending too much time playing tag with bullets with the Taliban, we'd risk missing our target altogether.

"Sierra, you and your team stay in the lead with first squad leading out of here. You can break off once we near the target." Sergeant Munn announced.

Keeping Mike and I in the lead allowed us to get eyes on any threats as they presented themselves. Allowing us to engage and eliminate them before they had a chance to pin us down and stall our movement.

0400 hrs.

The platoon continued with the mission, covering a good amount of ground, considering the circumstances. There were a few brief contacts with the enemy. However, they were short-lived. The fighters who did decide to engage with us were quickly taken out by the assaulters. Mike and I acted overwatch for the assaulting teams. Calling out enemy positions to the assault teams, so they could close in on and kill the threat. It was more of the traditional role of a sniper on today's battlefield.

The accolades of snipers I looked up to as a kid, such as Carlos Hathcock, would be difficult to find regarding the modern-day sniper. The Vietnam era's Snipers were used to infiltrate deep behind enemy lines and assassinate high-value targets. Some of the missions they conducted were even viewed as suicide missions. Conducting one of the high-risk operations, a sniper's likelihood of making it back alive was slim. Unlike today's snipers in the global war on terrorism, most of their work involved overwatch and surveillance. It's been said that the odds of a sniper pulling the trigger, operating in Iraq or Afghanistan, are close to one in one thousand.

As our platoon neared the objective, less than half a kilometer away, Mike and I broke away from the main element to set up a position to overlook the operation. Our destination was predetermined and less than three hundred meters from where we believed the HVT to be located. Before leaving our Kandahar base, during planning, I picked a building that stood out amongst others in the area. Looking at overhead footage and maps, I noticed the structure was taller than the others. Furthermore, unlike the typical mud huts in the surrounding vicinity, it was a semi-sturdy-looking structure of concrete and rock.

I was always skeptical and nervous about approaching a building with my two-man team. Being away from the platoon, I felt damn near naked. We did have an advantage over the enemy with our night vision but lacked in the weapons department. Our sniper rifles were much less superior than what the guys carried in the platoon. The majority of the assaulters had semi-automatic M4 rifles loaded with thirty rounds of ammunition. Others used various machine guns, each holding one hundred bullets or more.

Our sniper team packed far less punch than

the assaulters with my SR-25 sniper rifle and Mike's bolt action .300 Win Mag. If we were to come in contact with enemy forces while separated from the platoon, it could be catastrophic. Especially if there was a large enemy presence. The best weapons we had at our disposal were our tactics in stealth and observation. No matter how comfortable I was with my teams' skill in evading the enemy, being separated from the platoon took its toll on my nerves.

Approaching the building Mike and I would provide overwatch from, the environment was as calm as it had been all night. As we extended our telescopic ladder to climb, plastic clicks were the only thing I could hear. Everything else was a dead silence. Not necessarily a bad thing to hear at the moment, either. The past few hours were filled with increments of bullets snapping overhead, so quiet wasn't so bad.

I began the climb to the top of the building first. As the team leader, I felt that it was my job to clear the rooftop of bad guys if there were any.

And, if anything bad were to happen during this vulnerable act, I wanted it to happen to me. A couple of snipers in my unit on previous deployments, after a climb, found an armed enemy fighter waiting for them.

"One Charlie, this is Sierra. We're all set and in position, over." I called over the radio.

The rooftop was clear of any danger, and Mike and I were now overlooking the objective. Our vantage point gave us a perfect picture of the battlefield below. Like watching a chessboard from above, I could see the assaulters as they made their way toward the target building. That's at least how I liked to imagine everything beneath me. Derived from my childhood memories of playing chess with my dad.

The target building was encircled by multiple outlying homes, including a six-foot-tall mud wall around the perimeter. The only way to gain entrance was through a steel gate, held up with cheap, rusted hinges and padlock. In addition, moped bikes, blankets, and cookware such as metal pots and pans littered the ground where we believed our HVT to be located. Nothing unusual as the locals spent most of their time outdoors.

The building of interest itself was as ordinary and visually harmless as the area outside. Three small windows along its front and a thin piece of sheet metal for an entrance door. An inexpensive Master lock was all there was to keep it from opening and closing. Along the side of the building were garments strung across an uneven wire that functioned as a clothesline. And the interior of the home was just as dull and uneventful. A flickering light illuminated the home living quarters from what I assumed by candlelight. But unfortunately, it didn't reveal anything in terms of activity.

The small village and target building were as dead and still as the quietness of the night. So silent, in fact, that I believed that the HVT heard the commotion we caused on our approach and fled the area. Honestly, if the home was vacant, I wouldn't have cared too much. If the HVT wasn't there, it reduced the chances of getting into another firefight, and we could all get out of this godforsaken place.

"Mike, I got the target. Keep an eye out on our six and make sure no one decides to use our ladder and come up behind us." I whispered to Mike.

By the looks of things on the objective and its lack of activity, I felt comfortable that I could provide good overwatch for our guys below.

"Sierra, we are approaching the entrance to the courtyard now. We'll be going loud both here and at the entrance to the main house, so be sure you guys keep your head down." First squads squad leader informed my sniper team over the radio.

Going loud meant that the assaulting teams would be using explosives to gain entry. There was no point in remaining silent by picking a lock or climbing the perimeter walls. We'd made enough noise as it was. By now, the occupants had to know that we were nearby.

Laying behind my sniper rifle, I watched as

a pair of assaulters emerged from behind a building and approached the exterior wall. Both moved methodically and cautiously as they placed the first explosive device on the outer gate. A tightly wrapped block of plastic explosive, C4, with a long detonation cord that extended a few feet out of its end was used to detonate it.

"Set. Breaching in five, four, three…." The assaulters tucked behind the exterior of the wall, holding one end of the detonation cord. They were stacked one on top of the other in a single file line as the countdown began to the first explosion, broadcasting it to everyone in the platoon.

As the countdown neared zero, I quickly shifted my focus to the target building and observed the windows on its outer side. If there were any signs of movement, I wanted to alert the team below before entering the courtyard. Then, a bright flash, followed by a loud crack, and a deafening explosion, shattered the silence. A billowing cloud of dust filled the courtyard. I could hear sounds twisting metal and falling debris and rocks as the C4 charge destroyed the main gate and a large section of the mud wall.

"Good breach," I said to Mike, still maintaining a steady watch to our rear.

Below, the team moved into the courtyard, clearing the area with their IR lasers and floodlights. Still, there were no signs of movement or life on the objective. Even the outlying buildings seemed to be unoccupied. Regardless, I kept a keen eye out for the enemy who may be playing possum, waiting for an opportunity to attack.

Once the team established a foothold in the courtyard and it was clear, they commenced placing the second explosive device on the building's main entrance. And again, initiated the countdown. However, unlike the first explosion, this blast was much larger. "Holy shit!" I mumbled, and the concussive shockwave made its way from the building and into my body. It was a blast so powerful that it caused my teeth to rattle and vibrate inside my skull.

Seconds later, the assaulters from two

squads, first and second, made their way into the building. The explosion had completely blown out the door and a large portion of the area around it. Destroying a section large enough, the assaulters could easily make their way through, unimpeded by obstacles.

"One Charlie, this is Sierra. I have movement approaching your location from the west, over." While the assault teams cleared the target building, I caught the dark outline of someone walking in my periphery. A man was making his way from one of the surrounding buildings. He wore a light-colored perahan tuban, the traditional attire for Afghan men, consisting of a tunic shirt with long trousers and a hijab on his head. He crouched, walking curiously over to where the ground teams were located.

"Roger, Sierra. Is the individual armed?" The ground force commander asked.

"I'm not sure at this time. He doesn't appear to be or have anything in hand or on his person. Over," I replied.

"Roger that, Sierra. Keep a close eye on him. You're clear to use warning shots to keep him away from the objective. But, if a weapon is identified, you are free to engage. Over,"

"Sierra copies all. Out."

The warning shot the commander referred to was a non-lethal way to get someone to stop. A single round would be fired near or at someone rather than in them. Killing an individual who didn't present a threat wasn't only against the Geneva convention; it was morally unacceptable.

I wanted to keep an eye on the man, who continued making his way closer. Although it would take me away from watching our guys inside the building. Nonetheless, the unknown individual became my priority. In doing so, I asked Mike to pick up the task of making sure the assaulters were safe. With the lack of activity on the objective thus far, I was comfortable attacking our position from the rear.

The man advanced further and was now well within one hundred meters from the objective.

A distance I was uncomfortable with, especially if he were to detonate himself with a suicide vest. Still, I couldn't identify any weapons. He was also close enough to make out the expression on his face. Suspicious, however, non-threatening. But as the saying goes, looks can be deceiving.

"Mike, I'm going to send one at this guy over here. Who knows what he could be up to." I said to Mike, lying next to me.

"Go for it. I got nothing over here." He calmly replied.

Instead of putting my crosshairs on the man's chest, I steadied my aim in front of him by a few feet. I wanted the bullet to pass close enough to him that he heard the supersonic snap as it passed by his head. If he was hiding a weapon and decided to use it after that, my second shot would be meant to stop him permanently.

After firing a single shot, I focused carefully on the man's next move. Nothing. He looked as if he were frozen in space and time.

"Everything good, Sierra?" The commander

asked, calling me over my radio.

"Roger. I sent over a warning shot, and he stopped his advance, and he's standing with his hands raised above his head."

"Good copy, Sierra. We'll be wrapping up here in the next few minutes and prep for exfil. Looks like the target found a way to sneak out before we had a chance to grab him."

Mike and I kept a close eye on the guys below as they finished gathering any intel left behind by the HVT. While we didn't kill or capture our person of interest, the mission was far from being unsuccessful. We killed a handful of bad guys throughout the night. Killing these Taliban fighters meant that we carried out the assigned task. And that mattered above everything else. Kill as many bad guys in Marjah as possible.

Of course, getting our HVT would have been the cherry on top. However, not killing or capturing him is what came with the territory of hunting bad people. Hundreds, if not thousands, of operations came up empty-handed in the hunt for

Bin Laden. Besides, the odds of being on the search for our HVT again were pretty high. And the chances that we would eventually get to him were even higher. Overall, in my eyes, the mission had been a success. Even considering my missed shot earlier that night.

THE SONG OF A BIRD

The chirp of a bird sounded quite different today.
He soared; wings spread wide. Not a part of the
flock, he flew alone. Astray.

While I heard the song before, in the skies above, I
never took the time to listen, nor gaze.
His path is adrift. No set destination in sight. He
rode the currents of wind like a maze.

And as he continued to sing his song, the higher he went, my eyes fixed upon him to gather a closer look.
His body was bruised and damaged. I could read his features like a book.

The appearance of a battered winged creature. I pondered, what his song had meant. But the more I listened, I gathered all that was sung, every dollar. Every cent.

A lonesome soarer. With an appearance that's been through hell.
A fragile and everlasting soul. Encapsulated in a fractured, dying shell.

The higher he flew, the more of the song he sung. The more I listened, I felt as if we shared the same tongue.

He sang without words. Only vibrations from the

pits of his soul. His song was as pure as snow, with an underlying tone as dark as coal.

Notes that purified the air, like the smoke of sage. His song was powerful. It shook the earth beneath him, more thunderous than rage.
Why fly? I know that your journey hasn't just begun. The question arose from the tip of my tongue. The bird sung, "Because so many of my kind, down there, have died so young.

Somewhere between up here and where you reside, and our worlds collide. I once cried a song amidst the dark clouds of suicide.

So now, up here is where I'll fly, in my peace of mind. A time for me to sing. Unwind. Never allowing the world that was and now is, to intertwine.

So here, I'll stay, battered, beaten, singing songs of praise to outweigh my cries in the sky. It's all I can sing, not allowing my pain to magnify.

So up here, I'll fly. Sing, and soar. Closest to the Sun without visiting death, never having to fly, through that narrow open door."

NOTHING IS OVER

"Let's get it on!" Sgt. Munn said, pushing away from his desk, centered in the middle of the tactical operation command (TOC). There was an excitement in his usually well-reserved, professional, yet semi-monotone voice. One that rarely presented itself while he was in the presence of the guys. A tone that must have meant we had a good mission on our hands, and he knew his Rangers would get into some good yet one-sided action. The kind of action we needed. Especially when you consider that there hadn't been any over the past two weeks.

The guys in the platoon were getting antsy. We were sitting on pins and needles, waiting to get into some action. It felt like we were being pinned up in a cage, poked, and antagonized. Waiting for the moment that the pen would open, letting us out and sinking our teeth into the enemy's warm flesh and bone. None of us wanted the complacent rust of being stuck in our air-conditioned rooms to build for much longer. After heading out, nearly every night, sitting around the past fourteen days, twiddling our thumbs, felt like an eternity.

Afghanistan was the place every combat soldier wanted to be. Due to the enemy activity at the time, it was almost certain that you would have your shot at seeing combat. Especially in the area we primarily operated in and the enemy we were going after. However, the Taliban had seemed to take these couple of weeks off for unknown reasons. There were speculations about why the enemy had been so quiet, although no one was certain. Some believed that the Taliban were moving location further south to avoid the allied troop movement in the area. While others thought that they were simply taking a tactical pause to regroup and reorganize with more troops and equipment. While there was no way of knowing for sure, I was more in favor of the latter.

The Ranger platoon I was attached to was inflicting a significant amount of hurt on the enemy in the area. Along with conventional and allied forces, we definitely put ripples in the enemy's ability to fight. Since arriving in Kandahar, Afghanistan, almost three months ago, my platoon has conducted over eighty operations. Most of the work we were performing was taking down IED makers and Taliban leaders and groups in the region. On occasion, engaging with foreign fighters from nearby countries who filtered into our area of operation.

The fighting was intense, and the operations were some of the most eye-opening. Nevertheless, our platoon was intact and without suffering any losses. Well, besides my spotter, Mike. He left early after suffering an injury from falling into a hole. After a fast rope infill from Chinook helicopters, Mike unknowingly took a step off a ledge that no one in the platoon managed to see. As a result, he fell over seventy-five feet into a pit and smacked the bottom, full of cold water. The only thing that broke his fall was an old, waterlogged wooden ladder at the bottom. Thankfully, the only injuries he suffered were a couple of bruises and fractures in his tibia and fibula.

After Mike's early departure, I worked primarily on my own. I had a replacement spotter arrive from another platoon to help assist, but it was only for a brief stint. Our four-month deployment was winding down, and most Rangers from the other three platoons were returning home to the states. I'm not sure why our platoon was one of the last to leave, but I suppose it had to do with our mission success. Coupled with the fact that we were engaging and eliminating the enemy, almost every night, we went out.

This deployment was reminiscent of my first, to Iraq. But, unlike my first, and as the new guy on the team, I was more knowledgeable about the battlefield. The majority of our firefights were extremely one-sided. The enemy rarely knew what hit them when we started to return the hate we expressed so well through bullets and bombs. They would often engage us first, from concealed positions with a handful of fighters. But they were quickly overpowered and destroyed. This is primarily due to our superior tactics, weaponry, and ability to work well at night. As well as the three to one odds that we often had stacked against the Taliban. Three, and sometimes more, Rangers were locked in and prepared to kill one enemy fighter.

"Irv, take a look at what we got and start planning. We'll have a squad leader brief in ten minutes." Sgt. Munn said to me, pointing to one of the large screen TVs bolted onto the back wall of the TOC.

He referred to the squad leader brief primarily for those ranked Sergeant and above. It was designed to give the leader, those in charge of a team of Rangers, a time to hash out a rough plan before presenting it to our commander. Though the time allotted to plan was brief, it laid the foundation for our actions on the objective. There were five team leaders. One for each squad and our weapons squad. And the attached sniper team leader, myself, who always were in attendance during the brief. Each team leader conducted a specific role and task while in various locations on the objective. Our time to plan reduced the likelihood of us stepping over one another. Which could lead to friendly fire if we were to engage with the enemy.

On the TV screen, Munn pointed out, was black and white footage from one of the drones circling over a suspected target. The footage covered a relatively large area of space somewhere in the desert. I suspected it was somewhere near where we received most of our action, but I couldn't determine its exact location. Helmand province. Having good engagements with the enemy thus far, I figured the likelihood of conducting another mission there was pretty high.

From the drone's view, a large, square block of material was at the center of the screen. I figured that it was some sort of a glitch at first, but I wasn't too sure. Whatever it was, the drone had great interest. The area around the black square was what I believed to be anywhere from five hundred to eight hundred yards of open terrain. There were no buildings or structures that appeared to be in the area. Something I wasn't familiar with seeing, especially in and around Helmand. There were also tall palm trees that sprung up from the desert floor, making somewhat of a perimeter around the coverage area.

So far, based on what I was seeing, this mission didn't look too exciting and should be a cakewalk. My lack of excitement was also far less than what Sgt. Munn had expressed a few moments ago. Usually, there was movement in the targets we found interest in, and the environment had life to it. Those living in the area, including the individuals of interest, rarely knew of the eye in the sky above.

Even in less populated locations, there was always some kind of activity. A stark contrast from the target we were planning to hit later that night.

"Hey, Irv. I don't think you'll be closing out with more shots tonight. I heard this will be one of our last missions before we head out of this shit hole. We may have one or two more, but that's it, baby! Shit, I hope nothing happens out there tonight. We made it this far. The last thing I need is for one of us to get hit when we're a little more than a couple of weeks out." Sgt. Beck, third squads team leader, said as he made his way over to me inside the TOC.

He made sure not to make his announcement too loud to not gain the commander's attention in his office a few doors down the hall. Although, his baritone country twang was much harder to conceal. No matter how hard he tried. Beck, expressing how happy he was to be going home hours before a mission, was a sure way in getting reprimanded. In the eyes of a commander, this was a sign of complacency and not having one hundred percent focus on the task at hand. However, I knew Beck's was the exact opposite, and I felt the same way.

Being so close to hopping on a C-17, and heading back stateside, was on all of our minds. Most of the Rangers were already home from the platoons, deploying around the same time as we did. Most of us always felt a little on edge before returning home. A standing omen plagued our battalion regarding a deployment coming to an end. Since I was a cherry new guy, there was a belief that the odds of getting injured or killed on your last deployment increased significantly. It was almost destined that something bad would happen during a Rangers' final deployment. These odds increased tenfold in the remaining days and weeks we had left in a war-torn country.

Regardless of how the Rangers in our platoon felt, our mind was always on the mission ahead of us. We knew that performing to a high standard was the best and most sure way to return home safely. No matter how outrageous the platoon superstition may be. We never allowed it to affect our performance on the battlefield. Even though the thought did cross our minds every now and again.

"Anyways, dude, where are you planning on setting up your sniper team?" Beck asked as we both stared at the screens' drone footage, wanting to not let our minds drift away from the planning. He wanted to know where I planned to set up my sniper rifle once on the objective.

"And by a team, you mean one man." I jokingly responded.

"Yeah, you. I mean, look at this place. Nothing around to get good overwatch. You thinking of coming in with us or standing off somewhere?" Beck asked.

"Negative. The last thing I want is to interfere with your squads. So, I think I'll set up around the perimeter. I'll use what I can and possibly find some elevation on a hill or sandbur. But, by the looks of it, I'll be providing security to the objective's rear once you guys hit it. I'll cover the best I can until the ground guys get close, but my sight will be limited."

The team leaders from the remaining platoons began to trickle into the TOC, one by one. After waking up from a long, medicine-induced nap, some are still wiping the crust from their eyes. They all had a confused look as they watched the drone's footage. It was unclear what the objective was, as it lacked all of the characteristics of what we were used to. Nonetheless, we all were under the assumption that the mission would be an easy one.

"A cache!" Sgt. Munn stated as we walked into the TOC carrying a stack of papers in his hands. "It's a weapons cache, or that's what we suspect it to be, out in a field, buried in the ground. We've been tracking it for some time and believe it's supplying fighters in the area. It's also where they seem to ditch their weapons and artillery during the day or after an engagement. So far, we've seen three individuals come out to the location. They never opened the cache while they were out there. Instead, they were keeping an eye on it from afar, camping out under one of the palm trees."

"How do we know it's a cache full of weapons if no one has opened it, sergeant?" The squad leader of second squad asked.

"There's a high likelihood that it is. We've seen reports from units in the area coming across weapons caches similar to what we're looking at. In the center of the screen, you see nothing more than a black piece of cloth used to cover the caches' entrance. We know what they're using this cloth based on previous intel." Munn continued. He also helped shed some light on what I initially believed to be a glitch in the drone's camera footage.

We came across Weapon caches from time to time in Afghanistan. Usually, they held a few dozen or so AK-47 rifles, IED components, and the occasional rocket-propelled grenade launchers. While they weren't our main focus and something that we went after specifically, they were always cool to find and destroy. It was somewhat of a surreal experience for me whenever we stumbled on one of them. Seeing the weapons that the enemy has used, or wanted to use, to kill Americans. And knowing that if we didn't destroy them, there was a good chance that they would take the lives of my brothers and sisters in arms.

From previous missions during this deployment, enemy fighters tried their best to adapt new techniques and tactics to try and avoid our advanced technology. For example, to avoid being hit by missiles fired from helicopters and drones, they would wrap themselves in a blanket. This same tactic was also employed to not be seen by drones in the skies above. Taliban and foreign fighters picked up the belief that it somehow shielded them from a drone's infrared and heat-seeking cameras. A dark, preferably black cloth, would hide their bodies' heat signature, virtually rendering them invisible.

While the idea behind the enemy's concept was thoughtful, it didn't work. I recalled an operation earlier in the deployment, where two men on a moped tried the tactic as they were being tracked and engaged. An attack helicopter chased the two men near as they traveled down a narrow dirt road as they were fleeing the city. They must have known the attack helicopter would fire on them as they quickly leaped from their two-wheeled vehicle. As they tumbled and rolled into a ditch off the side of the road, they began covering themselves with a large blanket. As the helicopter approached closer, it fired two of its hellfire missiles at the two men a few seconds later. Needless to say, the blanket tactic had no effect, and the missiles did not miss their target.

"I want to be out of here and in the air on our way to the objective after sunset. Tonight's flight manifest will also be lighter than usual, taking essential personnel only. As you all can see, this objective isn't what we're used to hitting. Due to the lack of building structures, complexity, and location, there won't be a need for everyone to join."

Taking fewer guys on the objective was something that we did from time to time. I can only recall this on a handful of instances over six deployments. On a typical operation, anywhere from thirty-five to forty Rangers would conduct a raid. More than enough guys to raid a target or seize a small airport. But, on a mission like tonight's, twenty-five to thirty Rangers were all that would be needed. Having fewer guys was also a sure sign that we weren't expecting much resistance.

"You're about as light of a team as you can get, Irv." One of the squad leaders jokingly stated aloud amongst the group.

While his statement was an obvious one, a part of me wanted to join the list of guys staying behind for the mission. Hell, I'm sure most of us felt that way at some point or another. Having done so many operations, sometimes two a day, all the bodily pains settle in after a while. Coming off of a break from not doing much at all, the feeling of relaxation wasn't necessarily a bad one.

The mission brief was over fairly quick after Sgt. Munn gave us all of the vital information that we needed. Based on what we knew of the target, we expected it would be over in no time and should make it back in time for late-night chow. Squad leaders from first, second, third, and weapons, informed their men who would participate in the nights' mission and began prepping mission equipment. Those who would not be joining would stay behind and observe radios back at the TOC. In the unlikely case that shit hit the fan and we were in trouble, they would be the ones on a flight out to us and assist.

We had a couple of hours of prep time before we were to make our way to the airfield and head out. I spent the time getting my rifle, Dirty Diana, ready, applying a fresh coat of camouflage paint to her exterior. A light tan color for the base coat, followed up with light shades of brown and green to help break up the outline of the rifle. Since there were no buildings to climb and shadows to hide in, I wanted as much camouflage as possible, as I would be positioned at ground level. I was tedious in my work, carefully spraying coats of paint on Dirty Diana. If you were to ask any sniper, I'm sure they would tell you that it's a good bonding experience with their weapon. It was a time to further connect with it, as it was nothing more than an extension of our body.

Having the time to myself also allowed me to reflect on all we've done thus far this deployment. Where I painted my rifle out on the balcony of my room, it overlooked the larger Kandahar military base. The outdoor scenery was bathed in a dull, pinkish, and red hue as night drew near. Out in the distance, the rumbling sounds of fighter jets permeated the atmosphere. And as hostile of an environment we were in, the imagery provided a calming peace. As if the late, great Bob Ross had painted it. A scene that I often neglected to take in and appreciate when the opportunity presented itself. As rare as the occasion was.

A few thoughts crossed my mind as I sat outside my room, waiting for the paint to dry on my rifle. Being my last deployment before leaving the army, I thought mostly about my contributions to the war and those I served with. However, a part of me also wondered what impact we made. If any.

I witnessed a lot throughout my deployments overseas to both Iraq and Afghanistan. I was fortunate enough to have been there for the takedown of some of the worst human beings known to man. I was also deployed to see the innocent people of both countries free from the violence and horror imposed on them by various terror groups.

However, it never seemed enough regardless of who we took down or the territories we freed and returned to the locals. Every bad guy that we killed was always another to take his place. It reminded me of a deployment to Iraq when I was still a new guy on the team. My unit contributed to the death of one of the most wanted men in Iraq, Al Zarqawi, and over a dozen high-profile missions after that. In 2005, Zarqawi, using his high profile terrorist status, announced an all-out war against Shi'ites in Iraq. He successfully deployed hundreds of suicide bombers to attack civilians and American forces throughout the country. While we are unsure of how many lives he is credited with taking, it's believed that there were hundreds. One attack, in particular, was his contribution to the 2005 hotel bombing in Amman, Jordan. Zarqawi's contribution killed fifty-seven people in the attack and injured over one hundred more.

Then in 2006, while I was deployed to the region, his life came to an end during a joint force operation I was proud to contribute to. Although the excitement that followed after that was a short-lived one. By the time the news of Zarqawi's death made its way across the country and the globe, talks of another rising terrorist were emerging. One that had the same mentality, if not more extreme, than his comrade. And within a few short weeks, we were hunting down and preparing to cut the head off of the forever growing, poisonous snake that was Al-Qaeda. Unfortunately, those we helped provided safety and security after killing these violent groups returned to the same life cycle. They were doing the best they could, hiding in plain sight from those who only wished to cause them harm.

I wondered if what we were doing meant

anything in the grand scheme of things. Once the war was over, would there be another terrorist group uprising. Or individuals that were as equally destructive as those we were presently trying to erase off the face of the earth.

"Hey, Irv. We're all meeting down in the ready room and getting comms checks. So, I figured I come up and grab you before you miss your shot to get out." Erick, an assaulter from third squad, called out to me, making his way over to my balcony. He carried himself with the swagger of a suit and tie businessman and had a calm, Louisiana drawl in his speech.

I've known Erick for some time and deployed with him on all of his deployments. Separated by one year, Erick was my junior when we arrived in the battalion. We became good friends and connected right off the bat. Something rare for me. Especially towards the new guys coming in under me.

At times, I felt a little left out, not having a spotter and being the only guy representing the sniper element. It was easy to get looked over, not being a part of a larger element. However, at times, I enjoyed it. Being alone came along with the territory of being a sniper. It allowed me to be looked over for some mundane army tasks that the assaulters often endured. While at other times, like tonight, it made it easier to get left behind on a mission. Something that I would regret, not being there with my guys, and even more so if something bad happened.

I grabbed my rifle, which was now dry, and the rest of my combat equipment to meet up in the ready room. A short distance from the TOC, the ready room was where we made our last-minute preps before heading out. Like the TOC, the room was small. Made mostly of plywood, which managed to hold much of the day's heat that accumulated throughout the day. Making it feel like a mini sauna by the time we were all inside.

Most assaulters kept their weapons, body armor, and night vision in the ready room. As well as spare batteries, ammunition for each caliber weapon system, grenades, and C4 charges. Once everyone had the equipment, we would all perform radio comms checks. We made sure that all of our radios were in proper working order before we were on the ground, heading towards our target.

"You guys are taking incendiaries for this one, I see. I haven't seen those things used in forever, it feels like." I said to Erick and a few assaulters as I walked into the ready room.

"Nah, man, that's just because you're getting old. I carry one of these on me, on every mission." He responded.

"Well, shit. Make sure you and I are a good distance from each other. I freakin' hate those things. About as much as I do frags." I cracked a smile, responding. If getting blown up from a frag was bad, I couldn't imagine getting burned to death. At least, with the frag, I would assume it to be a faster death. Even if it was a mistake and one were to detonate prematurely.

Erick, carrying a pair of incendiary grenades, was far different from the standard fragmentation that each assaulter would bring. Rather than throwing shrapnel after it explodes, the incendiary produces intense heat through a chemical reaction. The grenade would be placed on equipment or a suspected weapons cache to destroy it in tonight's case. We rarely used them, but they were extremely effective.

Once our radio checks and equipment were in working order, we headed to Kandahar airfield and onto a pair of Chinook helicopters that awaited. The platoon was reduced to a little more than two dozen Rangers. Being in such a small element made it feel like we were a tier-one unit for a brief moment. Units like the notorious SEAL team six and Delta Force.

The flight to the objective was around twenty-five minutes. Enough time to try and grab a few minutes of sleep before things kicked off. My nerves were calmer than usual, as I didn't expect much activity once on target. My job was easy. Cover the guys from a short distance, less than two hundred yards. Keep the bad guys at bay, if there were any. As well as to cover the platoon during the exfil after the cache was destroyed. Based on the intel during the brief, the entire mission shouldn't last any longer than an hour.

While this wasn't our typical hunting bad guys mission, it felt good that we were taking weapons off the battlefield. Instruments of war that our enemy would no longer have access to and potentially threaten troops' lives and the locals in the area. During missions such as the one tonight, I felt like a difference was being made from time to time. Though small, I did take satisfaction in knowing that there was a potential, that we were saving someone's life.

"One minute!" The voices of the Rangers that filled the helicopter's interior shouted in unison.

As we approached the target, I took a look out the back of the Chinook's rear ramp. Again, the terrain was as expected. Plain, bare, lacking any signs of life, lonely. It was hard to believe that any form of evil could reside in the environment below.

However, I could understand why the enemy would want to use such a place to hide their weapons and equipment. The area was everything that you wouldn't expect there to be a weapons cache, let alone any bad guys. It was like hiding in plain sight, where less can be more, as it brings less attention to devious deeds.

Once the Chinook touched down and its wheels softly rolled on the dirt surface, the assaulters made their approach. I remained close to first squad, who was taking the lead. When we were within a few hundred yards from the cache spot, I planned to sit near the palm trees to watch them approach. We landed less than a kilometer from the suspected cache, giving us a tactical advantage. As open as the area was around us, it didn't matter how far away we decided to land. At night, the sound from two Chinooks, over open and flat terrain, could easily travel for miles.

Nearing the cache spot, I broke away from the first squad and set up my position to provide overwatch. I found a site underneath a set of large palm trees. Their fallen leaves and branches gave me good concealment as I lay in them. I felt like one of the old-school Vietnam snipers that I read about as a kid. It wasn't often that I had the opportunity to use such concealment. Most of the work special operation snipers conduct is from rooftops within urban environments. A location where the ability to hide is rare, and your greatest ally is being able to provide precision fire.

I watched as the platoon made their way closer to the target. An AC-130 gunship circled our location from above while simultaneously highlighting the suspected cache with its infrared floodlight. The AC-130 gunship also referred to as Spectre, is a ground-attack variant of the C-130 transport aircraft. We often used this heavily armed, long-endurance plane during our operations. It had the capability of raining down various forms of munitions, such as 20mm and 40mm rounds on the enemy from the skies above. As well as the widely known and devastating 105 mm howitzer. The Spectre was a flying fortress. Knowing it was on our side added a welcomed layer of comfort to all of us on the ground.

Besides the Spectre's vast array of artillery, it was also equipped with a high-definition infrared illuminator. A bright flashlight, only seen with night vision devices, shined down onto suspected targets. The Spectre would shine its infrared light down to further assist ground troops below when approaching an objective. Illuminating the target ensured us that we were heading to the right location and highlighted any potential threats not visible to us.

"Coming up on the cache. It appears to still be covered. We'll have the metal detector sweep around it for any IEDs before opening." First squads, squad leader, announced over the platoon's radios. The standard operating procedure was that at least one assaulter carried the detector, especially in an environment like Afghanistan. With every step you took, there was a potential that the ground beneath packed an explosive. If not an IED, there could be the remains of an unexploded landmine, leftover from when the Soviets attempted to invade.

I continued keeping an eye on the team as best as I could for the time being as they swept the location. But mostly scanning the emptiness that was all around them. The area was completely void of any activity. Honestly, this was shaping up to be one of the most noneventful operations of this deployment. It was sleep-inducing boredom.

"The area appears to be clear and free of any obstructions. We'll see if it checks out as a weapons cache and grab any needed photos before tossing in a few incendiaries." First squads, squad leader continued.

As the assaulters pulled back the cloth covering, I shifted my attention to our rear. My vantage point and what I could see behind us were just as bare and empty. Further in the distance, beyond the capability of my rifle, there were a few huts sporadically placed apart. Though, there wasn't anything for hundreds of yards that raised a concern or posed any immediate threat.

"Bingo! We have a cache. And it's a big one at that." The squad leader excitedly announced.

"Roger that. You and your team get what we need, and we'll prepare for an exfil out of here. I don't want to be here any longer than we need to be." Sgt. Munn responded before calling our Chinooks and preparing for an exfil to return to base.

The assaulters quickly took a dozen or so photos of the weapons cache. Once the blanket was removed, it revealed a wooden, four-by-four doorway that haphazardly covered the stockpile of weapons. Dozens of AK-47 rifles, RPGs, mortar tubes, dozens of pistols, machineguns, and thousands of rounds of ammunition filled a hole measuring seven feet in depth. Enough weapons to supply a decent-sized fighting force for a sustained period. One of the largest finds that I've seen throughout my deployments.

Once all the necessary photos were taken, Erick and another assaulter dropped their incendiary grenades into the hole. As they moved away from the area, the ammunition in the cache began to ignite and pop. This was caused by the intense heat from the grenade, cooking and melting everything within. The noises and hisses coming from the cache was the most noise we heard all night.

"Sierra, we're pulling back and setting up for exfil here." Sgt. Munn called and informed me over my radio.

The original plan was to have the Chinook helicopters pick us up a few hundred yards from the cache. However, the decision was made to move our exfil location, where the weapons stash was, instead. I assumed this was because we knew the area was secure. We've been on the ground for nearly an hour now. Without signs of a threat, our location was deemed safe.

I decided to stay in place rather than pick up my rifle and move to a different location. The helicopters would be landing behind me, closer to where the assaulter was, near the cache. Knowing that they had that area covered, I'd watch our rear, around the perimeter. No matter how safe an area appeared to be, our exfil always caused the hairs on the back of my neck to stand on end. More than I would like to remember, ex-filling at night sometimes took a turn for the worse.

"Five minutes out." Sgt. Munn announced.

While the two Chinooks approached closer to our pickup location, the Spectre gunship overhead suddenly began pulsating its infrared floodlight. It wasn't near the weapons cache, as it had been leading up to the target. Instead, it was shining a few hundred yards in the distance, near a pair of palm trees.

"Sierra, stand by. Spectre has identified one PAX (short for personnel) in the open, east of your position." Sgt. Munn immediately reported to me.

"Roger that, I'll keep an eye on him from here and pick up once helos are on the ground. Over." I responded.

You have to be kidding me. I said to myself under my breath. I was confused as to exactly what the aircraft was spotting. I hadn't seen anyone in the area. Not a single soul since being here. I was sure of it and knew that I had scanned the site a handful of times, using tactics taught in sniper school. Straight lines, color, shine, movement, etc., are the things that snipers are trained to look for when searching for a target. These characteristics hadn't failed me in the past, and I wondered how I could have missed someone in the open.

I shifted my focus and rifle in the direction of the Spectre gunship pulsating floodlight. Again, nothing. There wasn't anything in the area or under the trees as best as I could see. Regardless, I kept my crosshairs on the location, scanning left and right, looking for anything to stand out.

"Mike Charlie, this is Sierra. I'm not seeing anything. But will maintain eyes on and report, as necessary. Over." I radioed Sgt. Munn.

By now, the platoon was in exfil formation. It is positioned in a single file line, with every other man facing outward to their left and right sides. The helicopters were fast approaching as I heard their rotors thumping close by. Rather than staying in position as they landed, I slowly began making my way toward the platoon while watching the suspected individual in the open. At the least, I wanted to close the distance between myself and the platoon. Then, once the helicopters were on the ground, I would sprint onboard as the guys were loading on.

Then, out in the distance, I saw the outline of two Chinook helicopters against the night sky. A welcomed sight to see. Getting out of here meant that I could officially count tonight as one closer to getting home. By now, the helicopters were beginning to land. The floodlight was still pulsating over the area of interest, and it hadn't moved from where I first saw it. Regardless, I kept an eye on it while making my way to the platoon.

Snap, snap, snap! Green tracers flew overhead and in the direction of the platoon and helicopters. It was as if they emerged from the ground as they shot into the air. The shots were coming from where the Spectre's floodlight shined down on. Still, I couldn't see anyone firing. Only the tracers as they whizzed overhead.

    While I didn't have a shot at the individual, I wanted to do my best to subdue the gunshots. So, using the floodlight from the Spectre, I aimed my rifle and placed my crosshairs in the area. Then, in rapid succession, I began to fire. Sending one round after another until my twenty-round magazine was empty. I knew that I hadn't hit anything. However, the fire had stopped for the time being. Sometimes, the role of a sniper is more than providing well-placed shots into the enemy. In some cases, we can be used to cover fire for those we are overwatching.

    As I reloaded another magazine into my rifle, I sprinted towards the helicopter as the platoon filed up its rear ramp and inside.

    "Let's go! Go! Go!" Sgt, Munn shouted as I made my way past him and onto the aircraft. Munn was seconds after me as we quickly piled in, unsure if there would be another incoming burst of enemy fire.

    As our Chinook gained altitude and flew away from the cache site, still smoking in the distance, a bright flash lit the sky. Looking out of the helicopter's rear, we could see a plume of smoke rising from where we were taking fire. Spectre fired three 105 howitzer rounds from its side canon, killing anything within a thirty-meter radius.

"Dude! This shit will never get old, huh, Irv?" Erick shouted to me as we watched the deadly firework show as the gunship rained hate from the sky.

"Yeah, right!" I yelled back at him over the helicopters' loud turbine engines and rotors. Although, I could have gone without the last-minute confrontation on what was panning out to be a quiet operation.

We wouldn't find out until we returned to base and viewed overhead footage how the enemy was able to go unseen for so long. It turned out that someone was hiding in a shallow hole underneath the palm trees. We guessed they were there to keep an eye on the weapons cache. Or act as an early warning to call back to a larger force if their stash was discovered. None of us were sure why he decided to pick a fight as we were leaving. The cache was already destroyed, and we were leaving the area.

He surely didn't survive whatever his reasoning may have been, not attacking sooner, he surely didn't survive. The 105mm howitzer rounds sent pieces of his body and clothing feet into the air as they exploded around him. And as for us, there was a harsh lesson learned that night. It was always best to never plan for an easy-going night. Even during the final minutes of a mission, there's always a potential for an attack. Regardless of how close we were to the end of our deployment, returning home was never a guarantee.

THE PATTERN

"What do you think will come of this place. You know. Once we leave and the war's over?" I asked Mike. Both of us sat on top of our rooms' roof, taking in the Afghan scenery.

"Who knows, brother. We'll probably be fighting in some other country in a few years. Or shit, the next generation of warfighters our country produces will be. I just hope it's not back here or in Iraq. We've already lost enough if you ask me." He responded.

"I know, right? Call me a Debby Downer, but I swear this has to be what the guy's felt and talked about in Vietnam. Every time we kill the leader of some terrorist group, another pops up to take his place. Sometimes I feel like this shit will never come to an end. If there is an end."

"Who knows, man. But I tell you what, Irv. I sure will miss all this. In a weird, messed-up way. I'll miss taking it to the bad guys. Getting revenge for what they did to us on 9/11. I'll even miss you and some dudes who helped us out. Wonder what the locals will do once we pack up and finally leave here? You know haj will hunt them down and kill them and their families, more than likely."

"I know. Shit sucks, brother." I sadly, but truthfully responded.

History. It doesn't always repeat itself, but it sure does rhyme. That sentiment rings truer than ever these days. Moreover, this pattern tends to live up to its reputation, especially when the cycle is war. It's a pattern that can be traced back to the beginning of humanity. Since then, humans have always found a way to create conflict amongst themselves. Whether for territory, tribal disagreements, food, or even relationships, humans have a way of resolving their differences through acts of violence and war.

As a kid, reading books and stories of men who served and fought in the Vietnam war was something that consumed much of my time. After school, rather than finishing homework, I would sneak off to read what these fighters experienced in combat. I was absolutely consumed by what these men lived to tell. Unfortunately, my grades began suffering when opting to read Vietnam war biographies in place of homework. Nevertheless, these stories helped shape my dreams, which later became my reality.

Though most of what I read involved intense combat and guerilla warfare, I recall one story that stands out. It also has a striking similarity to what many men and women of our armed forces can relate to in today's wars. The fall of Saigon. A story that is less spoken of and glorified when discussing the Vietnam war. Perhaps, because it doesn't involve the heroic stories of battle in the jungle. Or maybe, because it sheds a little light on battlefield failures that present questions that some may find difficult to answer.

The fall of Saigon officially marked the end of the US involvement in Vietnam and the war campaign. The event took place on April 30, 1975. On this day, the Viet Cong, a communist political organization, and the People's Army of Vietnam took control of Saigon, the capital of South Vietnam. However, the events that took place days before are what I find to be most significant. Oddly, having a striking resemblance to our final days of the Afghanistan campaign in 2021.

On April 28th, 1975, President Gerald Ford received a note from his energy secretary while in a meeting. It warned that the South Vietnam capital was falling. Much faster than anyone had anticipated. Though most of the troops were pulled out of Vietnam under Nixon, US diplomats and service members still remained in the country two years prior.

Their positions were scattered throughout the region. Some lived on an Air Force base, some at the embassy in Saigon, and others lived in their own personal quarters and homes. In addition, thousands of South Vietnamese who helped the United States were also in the country. They all needed desperate assistance in fleeing before being overrun by enemy forces pouring into Saigon.

Much of the city was already surrounded and in threat of collapsing. Over one hundred thousand troops of the People's Army of Vietnam sealed off the capital as they made their final assault. The US administration faced immense pressure to evacuate any remaining personnel and refugees. A hasty yet risky plan would be needed to successfully evacuate those now trapped within the city. Thus, the President and Kissinger, the national security advisor, moved forward with a high-risk evacuation operation. This operation would be known as Frequent Wind.

On April 29th, the People's Army of Vietnam commenced its final attack on the capital. Operation Frequent Wind was now in full effect. Over American radio stations, just before eleven a.m., Irving Berlin's "White Christmas" began to play. This broadcast was the signal to Americans and at-risk Vietnamese to make their way to predetermined evacuation points within the city. The main evacuation point would be a joint service compound at the Tan Son Nhat airbase, the city's largest airfield.

Under the evacuation plan, helicopters would transport the remaining Americans and our Vietnamese partners to ships located in the South China Sea. Shortly, after noon, with the operation underway, buses moved through the city, picking up evacuees and transporting them to the airbase. Later in the afternoon, a CH-53 transport helicopter arrived at the compound on the airbase. By sunset, three hundred and ninety-five Americans and over four thousand Vietnamese were evacuated. Shortly before midnight, Marines who provided security and destroyed the classified files and equipment in the compound then began to withdraw.

While it wasn't in the original plan, a large-scale helicopter evacuation took place at the Saigon embassy. Thousands were stranded in the building, many of which were Vietnamese. Unfortunately, that number was much greater, with thousands of civilians gathering along the embassy's perimeter seeking to gain refugee status. Furthermore, adding to the difficulty of the operation, thunderstorms entering the area presented additional problems for transport helicopters. Nonetheless, the withdrawal of personnel continued well into the night and early morning.

By four o'clock in the morning, a determination was made by both Kissinger and Ford that only Americans were to be evacuated. The decision came amidst a growing threat that the North Vietnamese would soon overrun and take control of the city. As well as Presidents Ford's urge to announce to the American people back home that the evacuation of Americans was complete. Ford's orders weren't taken with much acceptance. And the pilots who flew the evacuating aircraft met the demands with some resistance. Despite some reluctance, the President's orders were carried out. Nonetheless, before sunrise, nine hundred and seventy-eight Americans had been evacuated around five in the morning, accompanied by eleven hundred Vietnamese.

The situation on the ground for evacuees looked grim at best. Heavy rocket and mortar fire continued to rain from the sky and around the base. The surrounding city was quickly beginning to crumble and fall into the hands of the People's Army of Vietnam. Much faster than anyone had predicted or prepared for. Any firefights and skirmishes that erupted around the city of Saigon were brief and offered only little resistance. By Operation Frequent Wind's completion, over four hundred Vietnamese and South Koreans were left stranded at the embassy. As well as those who gathered around its walls.

At the time, the air evacuation during Operation Frequent Wind was of the largest of its kind. However, it was also one of the biggest blunders since the war in Vietnam began. On the afternoon of April 30th, the city of Saigon was taken over and handed over to the communist, anti-government forces with little resistance to prevent further bloodshed. Shortly after, following the fall of Saigon, those left behind were sent off to re-education camps. Estimates are between one hundred thousand to almost a quarter of a million Vietnamese, and tens of thousands of informants were systematically killed.

After learning and reading the history of the Fall of Saigon, it seemed like it was copy-and-pasted over the Afghanistan withdrawal. The tragedies that unfolded as a two-decade-long war closed were broadcasted for everyone to witness. I found it hard not to watch, as it was hard to avoid the news coverage. But why would I want to avoid it? I spent a good portion of my young adulthood fighting in

Afghanistan. As I'm sure, it affected the hundreds of thousands of veterans across the board. Regardless if they fought there or not.

My world and how I saw it changed drastically after September 11th, 2001. I was in high school, taking a biology class when the news made its way to us that the Twin Towers in New York were hit by planes. Teachers and staff turned on classroom televisions and radios to get as much information as possible. None of us knew the extent of events taking place across our country. However, we all felt that we were witnessing history unfold before our eyes.

I remember rushing home from school and watching the news with my parents. A steady stream of news coverage displayed collapsing and burning buildings. Men and women leaping from the Towers to their deaths filled our screens. The day seemed as if it were pages ripped from a horror novel. They were traumatic, surreal, unpredictable, and will stick with most of us, if not all, for as long as we live.

As traumatizing as it was that day when terrorists attacked our country, I felt nearly the same shock and horror twenty years later. The date was April 14, 2021. In a statement to the United States, President Joe Biden announced that the deadline to withdraw troops by May 1st would not be met. A few months prior, the May deadline had been made between the United States and the Taliban during somewhat constructive talks. Under this arrangement, the remaining three thousand and five hundred soldiers would finally leave the country.

Instead of the May 1st deadline, the administration opted for a full withdrawal by the twentieth anniversary, on September 11th, 2021. In the meantime, the United States would function as a support role. US troops would not conduct any offensive attacks during this time and would do their best to support the peace process. It would be up to the Afghan security forces we had been training for years to take the fight to the enemy if necessary. President Joe Biden wanted the United

States' role in America's longest war to be over. Leaving as small of a military footprint as possible.

However, by August, despite the President's calls for a peaceful transition of power, Afghanistan was taking a turn for the worse. During this time, I began to tune in to the unfolding situation in the country I fought and lost one too many of my brothers in. I can vividly recall where I was and what I was doing when I saw horrific news coming out of Afghanistan. My state of shock was almost comparable to when I saw the televised attacks in New York and at the Pentagon.

"Heavy fighting in Northern Afghanistan, as Taliban closing in on winning their third capital." A stern-faced news reporter said as he reported live on air.

On August 8th, the city of Kunduz was largely under Taliban control. The same enemy that I spent years hunting, fighting against, and killing, were now gaining total control of the provincial capital city of Kunduz. Less than two hundred miles north of the country's capital, Kabul. The insurgent group had already successfully taken over Sheberghan, where an Uzbek warlord resided in the weeks prior. As well as the Zaranj, an Afghan city that is the country's major border crossing between Afghanistan and Iran.

Meanwhile, amidst the heavy fighting, the Taliban were also in the midst of taking control of multiple provincial capitals. Lashkar Gah, Herat, and the city where I spent my last deployment and experienced some of the most violent fighting of my career, Kandahar. The takeover of these cities was extremely strategic and well thought out by the Taliban. Gaining control of these cities put them in the perfect position to surround the capital.

Hearing the news of the Taliban's offensive advances was sickening and hard for me to digest. Let alone difficult to make sense of it all. The information out of Afghanistan poured in like a waterfall. And at times, my emotions felt as if they were going to burst out like a dam under extreme pressure. It was as if everything we fought so hard for was being given up right before my eyes.

"What the hell was all this for?" I said aloud, watching my TV alone on my living room sofa. The question burned me from the inside out and was hard to contain to myself.

With each passing day, my eyes were stuck to either my television or the screen on my phone. While I had been separated from the army for years now, I felt as if I were still in Afghanistan. There was a rage that boiled within me. I hadn't felt this violence since my boots were on the battlefield, taking the fight to the enemy. However, there was no enemy for me here to fight. No Taliban to kill. All that I could do was sit and watch the enemy destroy the lives of innocent people.

Then, on August 15th, my worst fears became my reality. Taliban forces seized the presidential palace and took full control of Kabul. It was reported that they faced little resistance from Afghan security forces, with some negotiating their surrender. I knew the probability was high from the events leading up. However, I continued to wish for a better outcome. After investing countless hours and billions of dollars in outfitting and training the security forces, I wanted more of them. The fate of their country and future generations would now be in the Taliban's hands.

United States government officials originally suspected that the Afghan government and security forces could hold out from six months to possibly a year. Instead, the resistance they encountered from locals and security forces was a lighthearted effort at best. It seemed as if the Taliban were nearly impossible to stop. Something that took one of the greatest militaries on the face of the Earth decades to accomplish, the Taliban appeared to do so in a matter of weeks.

On August the 16th, the world was stunned as we continued to spectate from the sidelines of the Afghan withdrawal. Kabul airfield, the main point of evacuation for evacuating Americans and Afghan personnel, became a place of utter chaos. Hungry and dehydrated, thousands of local Afghans surrounded the airport's perimeter. They were men, women, and children who wanted nothing more than to flee the country and from the certainty of the Taliban's rule. Some were Afghans who assisted the United States during the war. Providing us with valuable intelligence and fighting alongside us on and behind the enemy lines against insurgents. Without a doubt, they quickly became our allies and brothers in arms.

The security situation at the Kabul airfield was deteriorating at a rapid pace. Gunfire erupted from within the crowds, most likely from the Taliban, controlling checkpoints to prevent locals from fleeing. Thousands of Afghans were understandably in fear of their lives and did whatever they could to try and escape. As a result, the crews of C-17 cargo planes that awaited on the airports' tarmac decided that it was best to depart the airfield. Those who surrounded the airport, waiting to board one of the large transport aircraft, were in total disbelief.

Hundreds began to storm the airfields gates and checkpoints in a final desperate act. They hoped they would somehow board onto one of the

C-17s before taking off before they were left behind. Apache helicopters acted as escorts and deterrents for the cargo planes as they made their way onto the runway. They hovered and flew a few feet above the ground to try and prevent anyone from interfering with the plane's takeoff. The scenes looked like something I would expect to see as the world was slowly coming to an end. As if there was the threat of an asteroid impact, and human extinction was inevitable.

    Despite the preventive measures of the Apache helicopters and American security forces, the flow of fleeing locals persisted onto the airfield. Hundreds of desperate Afghans began clinging to the exterior of the C-17. They grabbed ahold of any part of the plane that they could get their hands on. Some climbed onto the plane's wings and its doors, all trying to find a way inside to safety. Others sought refuge by tucking their bodies inside the aircraft's landing gear hatches and compartments. Those who couldn't climb aboard were left running beside it, trying their best to keep up. Perhaps, praying that the plane would stop and allow them to board.

The C-17s continued with their exit out of the area to safety as Kabul airport collapsed around them. Their four large turbine engines revved and screamed as they gained speed down the runway. First, a few Afghans who held on for their lives were sent tumbling on the hot surface beneath. Then, as the plane climbed up into the sky, those who managed to still cling on began falling.

"Those can't be bodies…." I thought to myself, watching the footage shared millions of times over the internet by now.

I knew exactly what I was witnessing in the video. Still, motionless bodies began falling from the sides and underneath the C-17. It was a difficult image at first to grasp. It forced me back to the terrorist attack on our country on 9/11. In some ways, sharing similarities to those who jumped to their death as the Twin Towers burned. I couldn't fathom choosing between the options of being burnt alive or falling hundreds of feet from a building. Or being an Afghan wanting to desperately flee the country and feeling my only option is to hold onto the side of an aircraft as it flew away.

I continued watching the video in absolute disbelief. First one, then two, followed by a few more bodies that fell from the plane, hundreds, if not thousands of feet from above. One individual near the scene recalled that the bodies sounded like small explosions as they fell back onto the paved tarmac. Nonetheless, the planes continued climbing and gaining altitude. The aircraft that had not yet managed to take off were now in the process of taking off and faced similar circumstances.

After the footage raised great concern for anyone who watched, President Biden addressed the American people the next day. He went on to say that he was sticking behind his decision to withdraw troops. Also, standing firm behind his belief that the US mission in the country was over. And had been for some time. However, President Biden did acknowledge that thus far, the evacuation that he ordered had been "messy" and blamed the Afghan security forces for the issues. The President also announced that there would be an additional six thousand troops deploying to the country. However, he assured Americans that they wouldn't act in an offensive capacity. Instead, to help secure the Kabul airport. As well as helping provide aid in evacuating Americans and allies who were still trapped in the country.

During the President's August 16th address, he also promised a concerned nation our military would successfully rescue the Afghans who fought alongside us. As well as extending the refugee status to civilians in the country who were considered vulnerable under the Taliban. While the number of individuals seeking to flee would surely be in the thousands, he and his administration guaranteed a successful evacuation. Furthermore, stating that no one who sought to escape would be left behind. It is a promise that all military personnel understand all too well, regardless of their time in service. Everyone who has worn the armed forces' uniform has it pounded into them that no one was to ever be abandoned. Instead, we would make it our dying effort to bring everyone back home.

After President Biden's address, the six thousand US troops arrived in Afghanistan. Their presence appeared to have been making an impact at the Kabul international airport. Far from the chaotic events only a few days ago. The airport appeared to be under control and secure and allowed the progress of evacuees to leave the country. Although the Taliban fighters continued to surround the area, maintaining checkpoints, they let the US proceed in their operations.

That all suddenly changed dramatically, in a hard to forget and violent fashion the morning of the 26th. A large explosion rocked the area outside the Kabul airport, near one of the checkpoints where thousands continued to gather, awaiting evacuation. Reports of another detonation began to flood the airwaves and were reported across multiple news stations. Although, news of a second explosion was determined not related to the attack outside the airport.

Images and video footage of screaming Afghan men, women, and children were shown across television screens worldwide. Twisted metal and bloodied bodies lay across the ground. Women held their dying and deceased children in their arms as they cried to the heavens above them. All of what I saw was something I was far too familiar with while deployed. Suicide attacks from Taliban fighters and extremists against the innocent were what I knew existed in Afghanistan. These cowardly attacks and the devastation they produced happened from time to time during my rotations to the middle east. Unfortunately, they were a very real portion of our reality and what we faced, day in and day out.

As the news continued to cover the suspected terrorist attack, the reports of those killed began flowing in. From the looks of the devastation on the ground, I knew the death toll would be high. This was especially the likelihood in areas as condensed and crowded as the one at the Kabul airport. When an explosion occurs in a heavily populated place, everything in the immediate vicinity becomes deadly.

At first, the death toll numbered in the dozens. Then, a few more. I watched in shock as the number continued to climb higher and higher. Eventually, the number of Afghans killed crept over one hundred, fearing many more to have been injured. Then, the tragedy of the event took another turn for the worse. US officials announced and confirmed that American military troops were among those killed.

Thirteen United States service members, both men and women were killed during the blast.

"What are we even dying for at this point?" I thought to myself.

After all that we had been through, we continued to take casualties as a military. Those thirteen killed were not in a firefight or hunting the enemy. No. Instead, these men and women died protecting and helping those wishing to flee a country they no longer wanted to live in. And unfortunately, at the moment, there wasn't anything that they could do about it or retaliate. The president and his administration made it clear that they would not put troops in such a situation. They believed that ongoing operations and fighting would only prolong the US' stay in the region and further disrupt evacuation efforts.

This attack that killed the service members would be the first since February 2020. A shocking realization not only for myself but also for those who have served and deployed to the region. For over one year, the US went without suffering casualties as the war in Afghanistan continued. Learning about the recent loss of life felt like a blow to the gut. Not solely because of our brothers and sisters in uniform we lost, but also of the civilian casualties.

Later, it was discovered that the Islamic State claimed responsibility for the attack outside the Kabul airport. With this information, the United States felt that it had a reason for retaliation and an identifiable target. Furthermore, the suspect was said to be a plotter from the terrorist organization and lived within the city. Thus, the administration carried out an airstrike using the intelligence gathered over the days.

The airstrike was executed via an unmanned Reaper drone armed with hellfire missiles on August 29th. The drones had tracked the suspect, traveling in an old, beat-up Toyota Corolla, until eventually parking at a housing compound in Kabul. With confidence that the individual they were tracking participated in the attack, the order was given to attack. Then, just before five o'clock in the afternoon local time, a Reaper drone fired its missiles, striking the compound and truck of the suspect.

Initially, the strike was labeled a success, and the suspected plotter was killed. Although, these reports were immediately questioned as the locals reported a strikingly different story. According to the suspects' relatives, the man killed had no relation to the terror group. They also stated that he was not the only one who died during the attack.

Furthermore, his relatives provided photographic evidence that multiple children were also among the dead. They also said the man killed had worked side-by-side with the Americans. Helping to fight the terrorist group he was accused of being a part of.

The contradiction to the story America was first led to believe would be true. It turned out that the suspect, later identified as Mr. Ahmadi, was actually a contractor for the US. Moreover, during the withdrawal, Ahmadi had recently applied for resettlement to the United States, fearing his safety if he remained in Afghanistan. After further investigation and growing pressure, the Biden administration was forced to acknowledge their horrific operational mistake. In all, the drone strike killed ten innocent civilians, with seven of them being children.

August 30th, 2021

Through night-vision goggles, the image of

a soldier boards the last cargo plane leaving Kabul, Afghanistan. He carries his rifle in one as he boards, wearing an army combat uniform, body armor, and helmet with night-vision attached. This soldier is US Army Major General Chris Donahue and is the last service member to leave Afghanistan. This symbolic scene marks the end of the war in Afghanistan and our country's involvement in a two-decade-long war.

After an intense and violent two-week period, as expected, the President makes an announcement to the American people and the world. He states that there was a lot to be learned from the Afghan withdrawal's debacle. Also, our involvement in Afghanistan was the end of an era. It marked the end of the United States military, conducting operations to remake other countries from this day forward.

Two thousand four hundred one US servicemen and women lost their lives in Afghanistan over this twenty-year war. And a quarter of a million Afghans have been killed during the war since 2001. Yet, although the military operations were over in the country, and hopefully more loss of life, our mission was not over. While the evacuation was the largest air operation of its kind, rescuing more than one hundred and twenty thousand people, there were still thousands left behind. Despite the President and his administrations' promises. Most left behind were Afghans who helped assist the US and its allies during the war campaign and hundreds of Americans.

Along with those who remained in the country, the US was also leaving thousands of pieces of military equipment. The equipment ranges from tens of thousands of firearms, mortars, grenade launchers, armored vehicles, aircraft, and pickup trucks. All of them were left behind in Afghanistan, only to fall into the hands of the enemy. The thought that we were leaving so much behind made my stomach churn that I physically felt sick. Knowing that these were once the weapons that we once used to defend the lives of our brothers in arms and ourselves was heartbreaking.

For the next few days, I watched footage of the Taliban continuing to take control of the region and threaten the lives of innocent locals. The enemy I once fought now controlled the same lands that my brothers and sisters died for. And now, they had our weapons to help aid them in their cowardly advance. It was as if none of our contributions made in the time of war mattered. Like the political leaders who sent us to fight didn't understand or care about the sacrifices we made.

As I sit back and watch the country given on a silver platter to a terrorist group, I'm left with one pressing question. What was it all for? Although, I fear this question may never be answered.

However, I do have one desire. One that I hope benefits those after me. Those who decide to put on the uniform and sign on the dotted line. I hope that before we choose to partake in military operations, we take the precautions necessary to never repeat our history once more. To continue the pattern and the tragedy of war. Both during the campaign and after.

ABOUT THE AUTHOR

Nicholas Irving, a former Sergeant within the Special Operations unit, 75th Ranger Regiment 3rd Ranger battalion, served as an assaulter, machine gunner, designated marksman and sniper. He is now the *New York Times* bestselling author of memoirs *The Reaper* and *Way of the Reaper*, as well as runaway three part, hit thriller novel series, *Reaper: Ghost Target*. Nicholas is also a star on the FOX reality TV show *American Grit, a movie consultant of The Wall, actor on Master of Arms, and stunt double on CBS SEAL Team.*

Nicholas has six deployments with the 75th Ranger Regiment to both Iraq and Afghanistan and deployments to Iraq as a private military contractor. He is known for his position as a sniper, where he set a single record for a 3 1/2 month deployment to Afghanistan, eliminating 33 enemy combatants (as well as high value targets) with probable's unknown. Sgt. Irving was also the first African American sniper to deploy as a sniper within his unit to the Global War on Terrorism (GWOT). After his career within the special operations community, Nicholas Irving deployed to Iraq as a private military contractor.

www.ingramcontent.com/pod-product-compliance
Lightning Source LLC
Chambersburg PA
CBHW030109170426
43198CB00009B/555